Short Stories
from the
Bible

Short Stories
from the
Bible

Jesse Lyman Hurlbut

retold by
Colleen L. Reece

PUBLISHING, INC.
Uhrichsville, Ohio

Published by Barbour Publishing, Inc., P.O. Box 719, Uhrichsville, OH 44683 http://www.barbourbooks.com

Member of the
Evangelical Christian
Publishers Association

Printed in the United States of America.

THE STORY OF CREATION
Genesis 1-3

Our world is so old no one knows when it was made. We do know God lived long before earth or sun or stars existed, for He always was and always will be.

Long ago God spoke and formed the earth and the heavens. The earth wasn't as beautiful as it is now, but it was a great round ball with land and water all mixed together. Nothing could live in the pitch blackness or on the earth until God created light out of the darkness.

First, He said, "Let there be light," and light shone forth on the world, but part of the time it stayed dark. God called the two parts day and night and so was created the first day. On the second day, He spoke again. Dark clouds and the blue sky appeared. Then the water in the clouds parted from the water on earth. And God called the arch over the earth Heaven.

God commanded the water to come together in one place to form the sea. He named the dry land Earth, and shaped beautiful mountains and valleys upon it, and He saw that it was good. On the third day, God ordered the grass and trees, flowers and fruits to grow upon the earth. On the fourth day, He told the sun, moon, and stars to shine on the earth. So the sun shone in the daytime, and the moon and stars by night. On the fifth day, God filled the sea with fishes, great and small. He also made birds to fly in the air.

"Let small and great animals come to the earth," God said on the sixth day.

The earth began to be beautiful, with its green fields and bright flowers, and singing birds and animals of every kind in the forests.

God looked around. Everything He had made was good, but His work wasn't finished. The earth was ready for people to enjoy, but there were none! There were no cities, no houses, no farms or children playing under the trees. "I will make man to be different from all other animals," God said. "I will cause Him to stand up and give him a soul, for He shall be created in my own image. He shall rule the earth and all that is on it."

God took some dust from the ground. Out of it, He made man. He breathed life into His creation and the man became alive and stood up on the earth. God also prepared a home for man. He planted a beautiful garden on the earth where four rivers met; in fact, the garden was miles and miles bigger than any park any of us have ever seen. God called the garden Eden, which means garden, park, Paradise. God named His first man Adam and brought Him to the Garden of Eden. He told Adam to live there and care for it, to eat from the fruit, and to name all the animals He had created.

Adam lived all alone in Eden until God said, "It is not good for man to be alone. I will make someone to be with him and help him." God caused Adam to fall into a deep sleep. While he was sleeping, God took a rib from Adam's side and made a woman. Adam called her Eve and they loved each other and were happy in the garden.

God finished making the heavens and the earth and the sea and all that is in them in six days. On the seventh day, He rested.

For a time Adam and Eve lived peacefully in the garden. God walked and talked with them, just as we walk and talk with our friends. They knew nothing of evil or wickedness. It was important for Adam and Eve to always obey God's commands, so He said, "You may eat fruit from all the trees in the garden except one. If you eat of that fruit, you will die."

Among the animals in the garden was an attractive snake who said to Eve, "You will not die if you eat fruit from that tree. Nay, you will become as wise as God, and know what is good and evil."

The fruit looked wonderful. Why had God said not to eat it? Eve knew she should obey God, but she desired to be wise so she listened to the snake. She ate of the fruit, then gave some to Adam. Immediately, they realized they had done wrong and tried to hide from God among the trees of the garden.

"Adam, where are you?" the Lord God called.

"I was afraid because I was naked," Adam confessed. "I hid myself."

"Why were you afraid of me?" God asked. "Have you eaten the fruit from the tree of the knowledge of good and evil?" Adam told God that the woman He had given him offered him the fruit and he ate it.

Then God asked Eve, "What have you done?"

"The snake charmed me and told me it would not harm me, so I took it and ate it," she replied.

Then the Lord God said to the snake, "Because you have led Adam and Eve to do wrong, you shall crawl on your belly forever. I will put hatred between you, the woman, and all mankind. But one of her children will subdue you."

God told Eve, "You shall suffer and have pain and trouble all the days of your life, and I will multiply your sorrow in child bearing and cause your husband to rule over you because you led your husband to disobey me."

To Adam, He said, "You listened to your wife instead of to me, even though you knew it was wrong. You also will suffer. You will have to work hard to get your living from the earth. To have food, you dig out thorns and thistles and weeds, plant, and reap until you die. You came from the ground and your body will go back to dust when you die."

Adam and Eve paid a terrible price for their disobedience. God drove them out of the beautiful Garden of Eden and placed angels with swords that flashed like fire at the gate so they could never return.

CAIN AND ABEL
Genesis 4

Until Adam and Eve disobeyed God, there was no sin in the world. Time passed and the first woman and man had the first baby born on the earth God had created. They named him Cain. Later on, another baby came and was called Abel. The boys grew and worked. Cain raised grain and fruits. Abel became shepherd of a flock of sheep.

Having to work hard was not the worst thing about being driven from the Garden of Eden. The worst thing was that Adam and Eve were not able to walk and talk with God and hear Him speak to them. Now before they could talk with God, they had to build an altar of piled-up stones. They would place an innocent animal on the altar and burn it, to show that the sacrifice was not their own but offered to God. Then they would pray and ask God to forgive their sins and to bless them and do good to them.

Cain brought the fruits and grain he had grown. Abel brought a sheep he had raised. He killed it and burned it on the altar. God was not pleased with Cain and his offering, but accepted Abel's offering. Perhaps Cain's heart was not right when he came before God.

Cain grew angry and jealous of his brother. Out in the fields, he struck Abel and killed him. The first baby in the world was also the murderer—and of his own brother!

God said to Cain, "Where is Abel?"

Cain lied. "I don't know. Am I his keeper?"

The Lord said to Cain, "Your brother's blood is like a voice crying to me from the ground. As long as you live, you shall be under God's curse. You shall wander the earth and never have a home, because of your wicked deed."

Cain answered, "I cannot bear this punishment! You have driven me out and hid Your face from me. If any man finds me, he will kill me."

God promised Cain, "If anyone harms you, he shall be punished." He placed a mark on Cain, so that all who knew him would know that God had forbidden any man to harm him. Cain took his wife and went away. In a distant land, he and his family had children and built a city in that land.

ENOCH AND NOAH
Genesis 4-7

Years passed. Adam and Eve had other sons and daughters. Their children grew up and had more children. People in those days lived much longer than people do today. Today some of us live to be one hundred, but people in those days lived to be eight or nine hundred!

More and more of the people who filled the land chose wickedness instead of obedience to God's laws. Enoch was one of the few truly good people. He did only what was right and walked and talked with God. He lived 365 years, but did not die, for the Bible tells us, "...he was not, for God took him."

Enoch's son Methuselah lived 969 years, longer than

any other person who ever lived on earth. But there is no record that he ever did anything important in all those years God allowed him to live!

The world grew more and more wicked. God looked down and could only find one good man, Noah. Noah tried to do right things that would please God. He walked and talked with God. Noah had three sons: Ham, Shem, and Japheth.

God told Noah He intended to send a flood to cover and destroy everyone except Noah and his family. "You must build an ark," God said. He gave Noah exact instructions on how to build a boat large enough to hold him and his wife, their three sons and their wives, and two of every kind of animal, along with food enough to last everyone aboard the ark for many months. Noah obeyed the Lord, but the townspeople laughed at him. God shut the door to the Ark and those who wanted to come aboard could not, because of their wicked disobedience. When the flood came, only Noah, his family, and the animals he had brought aboard as God had told him lived through the flood that covered the earth.

When the water went down, the ark stopped floating and came aground on Mount Ararat. The door God had sealed stayed shut, so Noah released a raven. The bird found no place to rest and came back, for the water had not gone completely down. After a time, Noah sent a dove. It also came back. A week later, he sent it out again. The dove returned with a fresh leaf from an olive tree. A week after that, Noah released the dove again; when it did not come back, Noah knew it had found dry land.

"Come out of the ark," God told Noah and his family. "Bring all the living things." Noah obeyed the Lord, and life began again on the earth.

The first thing Noah did was to build an altar and give thanks to the Lord for saving him and his family. Then

God caused a rainbow to appear in the sky. He said that whenever Noah or those who came after him saw the rainbow, they should remember God's promise that He would never again send a flood to cover the earth.

TOWER OF BABEL
Genesis 11

After the flood, people no longer lived close together. They moved to many new places in the world and began to fulfill God's plan to settle the whole earth.

A number of people moved south from Mount Ararat. They built a great city, planning to rule all the people who lived around them. Soil there could be made into bricks, so house and wall building was much easier than in other places. The people got together and said, "Let us build a great tower whose top will reach heaven, so that we may be kept together and not scattered abroad on the earth."

The Lord came down to see the city and the tower. He, however, did not want all the people on earth to live together because the very wicked persons among them would influence the godly ones and lead them away from God. God caused the persons building this city and tower with which they hoped to rule the world to start speaking different languages, instead of the same language they had all spoken before. Unable to understand one another, the people stopped building the tower and the city. The city was called Babel, which means "confusion." Later, the city was known as Babylon, one of the great cities of the Bible. Many people formed groups according to their new languages and moved away.

ABRAHAM
Genesis 12-22

Even though great wickedness was in the land, always a few persons remained faithful to God. One was Abraham. When the Lord told him to go to the land of Canaan, promising to bless him and make his name great, Abraham obeyed God and took his flocks, tents, and families and dwelt there.

Abraham felt sad, for he and his wife Sarah had no children and they were old. God promised Abraham he would have many children. The old man believed God, even though he didn't see how it could happen.

When Sarah heard the Lord say that she was to have a child, she laughed. She was too old to have children. Instead of trusting God, she took things into her own hands. She sent her maid Hagar to Abraham, as was the custom in those days. When Sarah learned that Hagar was with child, she was mean to her and Hagar fled. But an angel of the Lord sent her back and she later gave birth to a son, Ishmael.

After a time, Sarah also had a son. She named him Isaac. Sarah couldn't stand having Ishmael around. She made Abraham send Hagar and Ishmael away. If an angel of God had not shown Hagar a well in the wilderness, she and her son would have died. God promised that He would make of Ishmael a great nation, and He did.

Abraham grieved for the city of Sodom, where his nephew Lot lived. He knew God was about to destroy it. "Will you spare the city for fifty righteous people?" he asked. When God agreed, Abraham kept lowering the number until God finally said, "If I find ten good men in Sodom, I will spare the city."

But not even ten good men could be found. Only Lot and his family escaped the city. God told them not to look back. As they were leaving, however, Lot's wife cast one glance backward and turned into a pillar of salt on the plain.

Abraham was so obedient to the Lord's commands, that when God told him to lay his beloved son on the altar for an offering, the old man prepared to do so. "Where is the lamb for the offering?" the lad asked.

"God will provide," his father said and laid Isaac on the altar. An angel of the Lord called, "Abraham! Lay not a hand on your son. I know now that you love God more than you love Isaac." There would come a time when God would give His Son Jesus as a sacrifice for all the sins of the world.

JACOB AND ESAU
Genesis 25-33

J acob, the younger son of Isaac and Isaac's wife Rebekah, desired the birthright of his older brother Esau. The birthright meant more possessions and the privilege of God's promise that Isaac's family should receive great blessings. Jacob had his opportunity one day when Esau came home hungry and tired from hunting and saw the food his brother had just cooked.

"Give me some of that to eat," Esau begged.

"I will if you will give me your birthright," Jacob said.

"What use is a birthright when I am starving?" Esau retorted. "Give me something to eat and the birthright is yours." He solemnly vowed to keep his promise. It was not right for Jacob to selfishly bargain food for the birthright, but Esau did a terrible thing in caring more about his empty stomach than his birthright.

Isaac grew old and feeble. Esau did not tell him he had sold his birthright to Jacob. He went to the fields to get an animal to make food for his father. Isaac promised to give him the blessing when he returned.

Rebekah loved Jacob more than Esau and wanted Jacob to have the blessing. She told Jacob to bring two young goats. She cooked them just like the meat Esau cooked for his father. Then she had Jacob put on some of his brother's clothes and cover his hands with animal skins so they would be hairy, like Esau's. Jacob went in to see his father with the meal he had prepared. Since Isaac could not see well, he touched Jacob's hairy arms and mistakenly thought he was Esau. So Isaac imparted the birthright blessing to Jacob instead of Esau.

When Esau returned, he found out what had happened. He cried bitterly, "My brother has taken first my birthright, now my blessing! Father, can you not give me another blessing?"

Isaac had already promised Jacob the richest ground and that he would be ruler. He said Esau would live by the sword and his descendants be ruled by Jacob's descendants, but in time they would break loose and shake off their bondage. Hundreds of years later this came to pass.

Jacob, fearing for his life because of Esau's hatred, fled. One night on the way to his uncle Laban in Haran, Jacob had a wonderful dream. He saw stairs leading up to heaven with angels coming down and going up. God promised that the land where Jacob lay sleeping would belong to him and his children. God said He would take care of Jacob both going and coming back. Jacob took the stone on which he had rested his head, set it up as a pillar, and made an altar. He called it Bethel, the House of God.

At Haran, Jacob stopped at the well. A lovely young woman came to water her sheep. Jacob drew water for her and rejoiced when he discovered she was his uncle Laban's daughter, Rachel. They fell in love with each other on sight, but Laban made Jacob work for him seven years before Rachel could marry her cousin. Then Laban deceived Jacob and substituted his other daughter Leah!

Laban said, "In our country the older daughter must

be married first. I pray thee, work for me seven more years and you shall have Rachel." Jacob was angry at being deceived, though that was just what he had done to Esau. Since, at that time, men sometimes took more than one wife, which people today know is wicked, Jacob agreed. He worked for Laban fourteen years.

At last he gathered his family and went back home, fearing what Esau would do. To his joy and amazement, Esau ran to meet his brother; Esau showed himself to be a kind and generous man who forgave the one who had robbed him.

THE SELLING OF JOSEPH
Genesis 37-41

Of the twelve sons born to Jacob, he loved the second youngest best, for Joseph was the child of his old age. Back home, he made a coat of many colors and gave it to the boy. Joseph's older brothers envied him because of it. They hated him still more when he had a dream that meant he would be their ruler and they would bow down to him. Nine of them plotted to kill him, but Reuben, another brother, said to throw Joseph into a pit, which they did while Reuben had gone to another field. Soon, a band of Ishmaelite traders passed by on their way to Egypt. The brothers sold Joseph to them, then sprinkled his coat of many colors with goat's blood and took it to his broken-hearted father.

The traders sold Joseph as a slave to a man named Potiphar, who treated him well and put him in charge of all his household. Potiphar's wife changed from friendliness to enmity when Joseph would not do wrong to please her. Potiphar believed his wife and threw the innocent young man into prison. Joseph had faith in God and knew that God watched over him. He remained cheerful and kind. Two years passed, and Joseph earned a reputation in prison for being good, cooperative, and wise in the interpretation of dreams.

At that time Pharaoh had a dream and called for the wise men to tell what it meant. They could not. Then the chief butler remembered that Joseph had interpreted a dream for him and how what he had said had come to pass. He told the king.

Pharaoh sent for Joseph and said. "I dreamed of seven bad cows eating up seven good cows and of seven withered heads of grain swallowing up seven good heads."

Joseph replied, "This land shall have seven years of plenty, then seven years of no crops at all. You must store up now for the famine that will surely come."

Pharaoh said, "Since God has shown you all this, there is no wiser man in all of Egypt. I appoint you to do the work and rule over Egypt. Only I will be above you." Pharaoh took his ring and put it on Joseph's hand so he could sign for the king. He dressed him in fine linen and the people bowed before Joseph. The slave boy who had been sent to prison without deserving it came out to be a prince, all part of God's plan.

JOSEPH AND HIS BROTHERS
Genesis 41-50

As ruler over the land of Egypt, Joseph did his work faithfully and well. He inspected the entire area and saw the rich and abundant fields of grain. "Do not waste it," he told the people. "Save it for the time of need. You must give the king one bushel of grain out of every five, so it can be stored against the coming famine." The grain was kept in great storehouses in the cities, so much no one could keep an account.

After a time, Joseph married, and he and his wife had two sons: Manasseh, meaning "making to forget" and Ephraim, meaning "fruitful." His two sons' names reminded Joseph that God had made him forget all his trouble as a slave and made him fruitful.

Seven years of plenty flew by, then came the years of need. Only those in Egypt had enough to eat, thanks to God's warning Joseph of the famine. When people came to Pharaoh for food, he sent them to Joseph, who opened the storehouses. People from other countries also came to buy grain. Among them were the ten older brothers of Joseph. Only the youngest, Benjamin, dearest to his father now that Joseph was no longer with him, remained at home.

Joseph's heart leaped within him when he saw his brothers. He did not tell them who he was; he wished to test them and see if they were as selfish, cruel, and wicked as they had been years before. He pretended not to know their language and had their words translated into Egyptian.

"You have come as spies," Joseph accused. "You wish to make war."

"No, no," said the brothers. "We only wish to buy grain."

Joseph asked about their family. He inquired about Benjamin and listened when they said in their own language, "Evil has come upon us because of what we did to Joseph many years ago."

"I told you not to harm him," Reuben said.

Joseph commanded his guards to seize Simeon and

bind him. "He will remain in prison while the rest of you take sacks of grain to Canaan," he said. "When you return with the lad who is your brother, I will know you are not spies." He secretly had the money they had paid for grain put into the sacks of grain.

Jacob was glad for the grain but refused to let his sons take Benjamin to Egypt. "Have I not already lost Joseph and Simeon?" he demanded. "If harm should come to Benjamin, I would die of sorrow." Yet all too soon the family used up the food from Egypt. Jacob had no choice but to send his youngest son, along with choice presents and more money.

Again ten brothers went from Canaan to Egypt. Again Joseph received them and turned away to hide tears when he saw Benjamin. Again he ordered the asses to be loaded with grain, along with the money the brothers had paid. This time he had his silver cup put in Benjamin's sack, then sent his steward after them.

"You have stolen my master's silver cup," the steward accused and brought them all back to Joseph.

"He shall be my slave," Joseph declared. "The rest of you may go."

Judah, who had urged his brothers to sell Joseph to the Ishmaelites, fell to his knees. "Father Jacob loves Benjamin most. I promised to bear the blame if the lad was not brought safely home. I will stay as a slave. For you to keep Benjamin will kill Father."

Joseph knew at last his brothers were no longer wicked. One was even willing to suffer so his brother might be spared. Joseph sent away his servants and cried, "I am Joseph. Do not be afraid. God allowed me to come here so I might save your lives. Go home. Bring our father and all the family, for only that way can they be saved from famine." He kissed his brothers and wept, then sent wagons to Canaan to bring the father he had not seen in many years.

How great was Jacob's joy when he at last beheld the son he had believed dead for so long! He lived to be almost 150 and blessed Joseph's sons before he died. Joseph lived to be 110. He was not buried in Egypt, but was embalmed, put in a stone coffin, and taken to the land of Goshen with the people of Israel. Later, when God brought them out of Egypt, the children of Israel carried Joseph's bones with them.

A BABY SAVED
Exodus 1-2

Some time after Joseph's death, a new king of Egypt feared the Israelites would soon become greater than the Egyptians. He set harsh rulers over the people and laid heavy burdens on them. He took more and more of their crops. He also ordered all the boy babies to be killed.

One mother hid her newborn child as long as she could, then made a tiny, waterproof basket, or "ark," put her son in it and let it float down the river to where the daughter of the new Pharaoh would see it. "Hide and watch," she told her twelve-year-old daughter Miriam.

The princess saw the ark containing the beautiful baby boy and sent a maid to fetch it. "It is one of the Hebrew children. I will not let him die."

Miriam quickly ran to the princess. "Shall I find a Hebrew woman to nurse and care for the baby?" When Pharaoh's daughter nodded, Miriam brought her own mother! She took her son home and cared for him, knowing no one could harm him for he was protected by the princess of Egypt.

A BURNING BUSH
Exodus 2-4

When the child was large enough to leave his mother, Pharaoh's daughter took him to the palace and named him Moses, because he was drawn from the water. He learned much from the Egyptians, but loved his own people, the Israelites. They served the Lord God, while the Egyptians bowed down to oxen, cats, and snakes.

Moses left the palace and its riches, knowing God wanted him to lead the Israelites and set them free. They did not believe him. Moses got in trouble with the Pharaoh, and fled to a country in Arabia called Midian. There he helped some young women who brought their flocks to water at the well. They were daughters of Jethro, a priest. Moses stayed with them, married one of the daughters, and became a shepherd.

Many years later, he was feeding his flock on a mountain called both Mount Horeb and Mount Sinai. "Why, what is that?" Moses rubbed his eyes and stared. A bush seemed to be on fire, but it did not burn up! He went closer.

"Moses, Moses, do not come near. Take off your shoes, for you are standing on holy ground," a voice called from the bush.

Moses obeyed. The voice went on. "I am the God of your father, the God of Abraham, Isaac, and Jacob. I have seen the wrongs and cruelty My people have suffered in Egypt and I have heard their cry. I am coming to set them free and bring them to their own good land of Canaan. I will send you to Pharaoh and you shall lead My people from Egypt."

Moses asked, "When I go, they will want to know who sent me."

God said, "My name is 'I AM,' the One who is always living. Tell your people 'I AM' has sent you. Say to Pharaoh, 'Let my people go.' At first, he will not do this, but later he will, and the people will follow you."

Moses asked for a sign from God to give to his people and the Egyptians. God told Moses to throw his shepherd's staff on the ground. It became a snake. When Moses picked it up as God told him to, it became a rod again. God also gave Moses a second sign, changing his hand to pure white and scaly like a leper's, then back to normal. He promised Moses, who stuttered, that his brother Aaron who even then was coming to Moses in the wilderness, would speak for him.

TERRIBLE PLAGUES
Exodus 5-12

Pharaoh did not free the Israelites when Moses went to him. Instead he ordered still harder tasks. The people complained, saying Moses had made their suffering worse. Terrible things called plagues came upon the land because of Pharaoh's stubbornness: water turned to blood, so there was none to drink. Armies of frogs, lice, fleas, and flies attacked; disease killed the animals. People got boils. Hail—something the Egyptians had never seen—ruined the crops. Locusts ate every green thing spared by the hail. Three days of darkness fell, black and terrifying.

Still Pharaoh refused to give in. He told Moses, "If I ever see you again, I will have you killed."

"So be it," Moses replied.

God told Moses there would be one more plague, so

terrible that Pharaoh would be glad to let the Israelites go. The oldest child of all the Egyptians would die, but the Israelite families' eldest child would live. God told them how to avoid the plague coming at midnight. Moses said, "Each family is to kill a lamb and sprinkle some of its blood at the entrance to the house, the door frame overhead, and on each side. You are to roast the lamb, cook some vegetables, and eat standing around the table. You must be wearing your garments, ready to march away as soon as the meal is ended. Do not go out of your house on this night, for God's angel will be out and you might be killed if the angel should meet you."

The children of Israel did as commanded. They called it the "Passover Supper" because the angel of death passed over the marked houses. (In memory of that night, many Jewish people still eat such a supper on the same night each year.)

Pharaoh sent a messenger to Moses and Aaron after he saw his oldest son lying dead. "Make haste. Get out of the land. Take everything you have! And pray to your God to have mercy on us and do us no more harm."

THE RED SEA
Exodus 12-15

After 430 years in Egypt, the Israelites began their long journey home, marching family by family, tribe by tribe. They went in such a hurry they left their bread dough rising in the pans, setting them on their heads as people do in that land when they carry loads. The Lord went before them by day in a pillar of a cloud, by night in a pillar of fire, but when they came to the Red Sea, they discovered Pharaoh had gone back on his promise. He had sent soldiers and chariots to find the people who had done so much work as slaves.

"Here we are with a sea in front of us, our enemies behind us," the people cried. "Better to serve the Egyptians than to die here in the wilderness!"

"Fear not," said Moses. "Stand still and see how God will save you." That night a pillar of fire and of cloud stood between them and their enemies. A mighty wind arose, sent by God. It blew all night and by the morning, a path of dry land had formed right in the middle of the sea! The Israelites crossed over into the wilderness on the other side.

"After them!" the Egyptian leaders of the army cried. Chariots and horses surged forward, but the sand grew soft. The horses mired. From the other side, Moses again obeyed God and raised his hand. A great tide of water returned and covered Pharaoh's army, on the very path the Israelites had walked. Horses and men were drowned in the sea. The Israelites gave thanks to God for saving them.

MANNA FROM HEAVEN
Exodus 16

So many people needed much food. When they ran out, God told them, "I will rain bread from heaven upon you. You shall gather it every day." The next morning white flakes like snow or frost covered the ground. The Israelites said, "Manhu?" meaning, "What is it?" They called the food manna. Every morning the people gathered enough for that day, and on the sixth day, they also gathered enough for the seventh, which was the Sabbath. No manna fell on the Sabbath.

THE TEN COMMANDMENTS
Exodus 19-20

When the travelers reached the plain by Mount Sinai, the mountain trembled and shook. Smoke, clouds, and lightning covered it. Thunder rolled and crashed.

The people fell to the ground in fear.

God spoke in a voice of thunder, "I am the Lord, your God, who brought you out of bondage in the land of Egypt." Then God called Moses up to the top of the mountain. Moses stayed for forty days and God gave him two flat stone tablets, on which God had written the Ten Commandments.

THE GOLDEN CALF
Exodus 32-34

While Moses was with God on the mountain, the people grew wicked. They begged Aaron to make them a god to worship and lead them, for they did not know what had become of Moses. Aaron finally gave in. He took the people's gold earrings, melted them and made a golden calf; then he built an altar before it. He said, "Tomorrow will be a feast to the Lord."

Instead, they offered sacrifices and danced around the golden calf, doing wicked things, in spite of the smoking mountain almost above their heads!

The Lord sent Moses back to the camp. "They have made an idol and I am angry, ready to destroy them all," He said.

Moses pleaded with the Lord, then hurried down the mountain. Joshua had waited on the side of the mountain. He said, "I hear the noise of war in the camp. Nay, it is singing." When they reached the camp, Moses was so angry at what he saw, he hurled the stone tablets God had given him and broke them on the rocks. Why keep the tablets of stone when the people had already broken the laws written on them? Moses tore down the golden calf, smashed it, burned it in the fire, and ground it to powder. He put the powder in the water and made the people drink the dirty liquid as punishment for their wicked deeds. He scolded Aaron terribly, then called for those on the Lord's side to come stand with him. The whole tribe of Levi came.

Moses ordered them to kill all who had bowed down to the idol, and they did so.

"You have sinned greatly," Moses told the others. He went to the Lord, prayed before Him, and asked forgiveness for his people. God forgave them and Moses again brought the word of the Lord carved on stone tablets. His face shone so from talking with the Lord, he had to cover it with a veil because the people could not bear its brightness.

THE SCAPEGOAT
Leviticus 16

The people in the time of Moses worshipped differently than Christians today, for Jesus had not yet come to earth. Even the high priest could only enter the Holy of Holies (the inner room of the Tabernacle, which was a beautiful half-tent, half-house) on one day a year, called the Day of Atonement. The service that day showed people that all are sinners and everyone must ask God to take his sins away. This information is in the Bible, but there were no Bibles then and few could read.

On the Day of Atonement, two goats were brought to the priest after he had performed certain duties in the Holy of Holies. The goats were looked on as bearing the sins of the people. On the forehead of one goat was written, "For the Lord." It became a sacrifice.

The high priest came out of the Tabernacle and laid his hands on the goat called the scapegoat, whose forehead was marked, "To be sent away." This goat was led so far into the wilderness he could never find his way back, then set free. This goat represented the sins of the people that were taken away, never to return.

God ordered these goats as examples to help the people recognize that sin is terrible. It separates us from God and brings death. Long before Christ came to take away mankind's sins by His death, God showed men the way of forgiveness and peace.

THE SPIES
Numbers 13-14

After a year at Mount Sinai, the cloud over the Tabernacle rose, a sign for the Isrealites to move. They went to Kadesh-barnea, between Canaan and the desert. God told Moses to send men to look it over, a dangerous job.

Moses chose one man from each tribe, including his helper Joshua and Caleb of the tribe of Judah to spy out the land. Forty days later they came back with glowing reports, "It is a rich land, with grass for all our flocks, and fields where we can raise grain, truly a land flowing with milk and honey. But the people are giants, strong and war-like. Their city walls almost reach the sky."

Caleb admitted it was true but said that God would help the Israelites. Only Joshua agreed. The other spies said it was impossible to take the walled cities. This frightened the people. Here on the very border of Canaan, the Promised Land, they were afraid to enter. They forgot how many times God had already helped them.

All night they cried out against Moses, threatening to stone and kill Joshua and Caleb. Suddenly the glory of the Lord, which stayed in the Holy of Holies, flashed out and shone from the door of the Tabernacle and on the people's faces. God told Moses, "How long will this people disobey and despise me? None of them save Caleb and Joshua, who have been faithful to me, shall enter into this land I have promised them. All of the people who are twenty years and over shall die in the desert. Their children shall grow up in the wilderness and go into the land when they are grown. Moses, turn back to the desert and stay there until this generation has died. At that time, Joshua shall lead your children into Canaan. Caleb shall also go into the land and have his choice of homes there."

The people rebelled. They rushed up the mountain although Moses told them they must not go, for God would not go before them. "You are not fit," he cried.

They ran on, a mob of untrained men. Not until many of their number were killed by the people in that part of the land did the others obey the Lord and Moses and stay forty years in the wilderness.

MOSES DISOBEYS GOD
Numbers 20; Deuteronomy 31-34

When the forty years were almost over, the people came back to Kadesh but found no water. God told Moses to gather the people, and to speak to a great rock from which water would gush forth. Instead, Moses spoke angrily to the people, then struck the rock twice with his rod.

Moses' disobedience cost him and Aaron dearly. God said, "Because you did not show honor to me by doing as I commanded, neither of you shall enter the land I have promised to the children." A single act of disobedience cost them the privilege of leading the people into their own land!

Just before Moses died, he gave Joshua charge of the people. Then all alone, he went out of the camp and climbed to the top of Mount Nebo. He looked at the Promised Land, then lay down on the mountaintop and died. God Himself buried Moses, who had served Him so faithfully. After him, no man ever lived so near to God and talked with God so freely, until Jesus Christ, the Son of God came.

JOB
Book of Job

Some time in those early days, a good man named Job lived in the land of Uz. He was the richest man in the east, for he owned thousands of sheep, camels, oxen, and asses.

Job prayed to God every day, served Him and tried to live for Him the best he could. He even made offerings on his altar for each of his sons and daughters for fear they had sinned or turned away from God in their hearts.

Satan came and stood among the angels of God, as though he were one of them. He told the Lord he had been going up and down the earth looking at the people. When God asked Satan if he had seen how perfect Job was, Satan sneered, asking, "Does Job fear God for nothing? You have blessed and protected him. If you should take all he has, Job will turn away and curse you."

The Lord gave Satan permission to do anything he wanted to Job's family and possessions but he could not touch Job. Satan laughed gleefully and went off to do his worst. In one single day, Job lost all he had: flocks, cattle, sons, and daughters. Satan waited for him to curse God. Instead, Job fell down on his face before the Lord and said, "The Lord gave and the Lord has taken away. Blessed be the name of the Lord." To Satan's dismay, the man he persecuted neither turned away from God nor blamed Him for his misfortune. Job remained true even when Satan struck him with terrible, painful boils all over his body. He sat down in the ashes in great pain, but did not speak a single word against God.

"Why try to serve God?" his wife asked. "You may as well curse Him and die."

Job only replied, "You speak foolishly. Shall we take good things from the Lord and not take evil things also?"

Three friends, Eliphaz, Bildad, and Zophar, came to visit Job. Instead of cheering Job up, they made him feel worse by telling him he had brought all the bad things on himself by sinning. (In those times, most people believed trouble, sickness, the loss of friends or possessions were God's punishments for wickedness.)

Job shook his head. He had done no wrong. He might

not understand God's ways, but he would not blame Him. Job continued to faithfully serve God. After a time, the Lord gave Job more than he had lost: twice as many sheep, oxen, camels, and asses, and also seven more sons and three daughters, who were the loveliest in all the land. Job lived a long time with riches, honor, and goodness under God's care.

THE SCARLET CORD
Joshua 1-2

God spoke to Joshua after the death of Moses, while the children of Israel camped on the east bank of the river Jordan. "You are to take Moses' place and rule this people. Don't wait. Lead them across the river Jordan and conquer the land I have given to them." God said the Israelites were to have a great section of land, if they showed themselves worthy of it. He told Joshua, "Be strong and of a good courage. I will be with you, as I was with Moses. Constantly read the book of the law that Moses gave you and be careful to obey it, that you might have good success."

Joshua ordered his officers to go through the camp and tell the people to prepare food for a journey. "In three days we will pass over the Jordan and go into the land the Lord has promised us," he said.

The officers looked amazed. At that time of year, the Jordan ran over its banks, swift and deep and wide down to the Dead Sea. No one could possibly walk through it. Only the strongest man could swim it and the Israelites had no boats. They could see the high walls of the city of Jericho across the raging river. Jericho had to be taken before the rest of the land could be won, for it stood beside the road leading up to the mountain country.

Joshua chose two brave and cunning men to spy out Jericho. He told them to come back in two days. The men plunged into the swollen river, swam across, and went into Jericho. Unfortunately, they were seen and the king of Jericho sent men to take them prisoner.

Joshua's men ran to a wall in the city where a woman named Rahab lived. Rahab took them to the roof of the house and covered them with long, reed-like stalks of flax. Although she hid them, they had been seen going into her house. The officers who searched her house could not find the Israelite spies and went away, thinking those they sought had left the city.

Rahab told the men she had helped, "All of us in Jericho know your God is mighty and terrible and that He has given you this land. We heard how your God dried up the Red Sea, led you through the desert, and gave you victory over your enemies. All the people in the city fear you and know God will give you this city and all the land.

"Promise me in the name of the Lord, that you will spare my life, the lives of my father and mother, brothers and sisters when you take this city."

The men said, "We will pledge our lives for yours. No harm will come to you, for you saved our lives."

Rahab's house was built on the wall of the city. She let down a rope of scarlet from one of the windows. The men could slide down it to the ground. The two spies said, "When our men come to take the city, be sure to hang this scarlet cord out the window. Bring all your family into the house and keep them here.

"We will tell our men no one in the house with the scarlet cord is to be harmed."

CROSSING THE JORDAN
Joshua 3-4

T he spies told Joshua, "Truly the Lord has given us all the land. The people in it fear us and will not dare oppose us."

Joshua commanded the people to take their tents and move to the bank of the Jordan. The priests carried on their shoulders the Ark of the Covenant, a wooden box covered inside and outside with plates of decorated gold. It held the stone tablets on which the Ten Commandments were written and was kept in the Holy of Holies portion of the Tabernacle. The Ark contained God's Presence and a covering hid it from sight of the people.

"Walk into the water," Joshua ordered. The priests did so. A strange thing happened. The river above them stopped flowing, even though they could see the water far up the river rising and piling into a great heap. Below them it ran on, leaving a great dry place, with stones in the riverbed uncovered.

Joshua had the priests stand in the middle of the dry place and all the people passed safely over. Then their leader called for a man from each tribe. "Go into the river and bring up twelve stones, as large as you can carry, from where the priests are standing."

They obeyed. With these stones, Joshua made a pile on the bank. He said, "When your children ask about the stones, you are to say to them, 'Here the Lord God made the river dry before the Ark of the Covenant so the people could cross over into the land that God had promised their fathers.'"

Joshua commanded the twelve men to bring twelve more stones and heap them up in the bed of the river where the priests stood with the Ark. They would remind anyone who saw them of God's wonderful help to his people. When this had been done, Joshua told the priests, "Come up from the river and bring the Ark to the shore." They came and the waters again flowed down from above. Soon the river rolled on as it had before.

The people set up a new camp, from which to go forth and win the land of Canaan.

THE FALL OF JERICHO
Joshua 5-6

The Israelites came into Canaan at the time of early harvest. They gathered abundant grain and barley, ground it, and made bread of it. The manna God had sent from the sky through forty years was no longer needed and ceased to fall.

Joshua went out to look at the city of Jericho and its strong walls. An armed man came toward him. "Are you on our side or an enemy?" Joshua boldly asked.

"I have come as captain of the Lord's army," the man answered.

Joshua saw he was an angel of the Lord and bowed down, asking, "What word has my Lord to his servant?"

"Take off your shoes, for the ground where you are standing is holy."

Joshua obeyed. The one speaking was not merely an angel, but the Lord Himself, appearing as a man. The Lord told Joshua He would destroy the city of Jericho before him and told Joshua what to do.

For seven days, the Israelites did as the Lord commanded. Soldiers led the way. Priests blowing loud and long on trumpets of rams' horns followed, then the Ark of the Covenant on the shoulders of other priests. The army of Israel came last. No one shouted or made any noise, except for the sound of the trumpets. Each morning for six days they formed in the same order and marched around the city.

On the seventh day, they rose very early. This time they marched around the city wall not just once, but seven times, then stood still. The trumpets ceased. Into the great silence came Joshua's order, "Shout, for the Lord has given you the city!"

The people shouted. They looked at the wall. It trembled, shook, and fell flat to the ground except for the place where a scarlet cord hung from the window! Joshua ordered the two spies Rahab had saved to bring her and her family out where they would be safe. They would be cared for in camp until war against the people of the land ended.

Rahab, who saved the spies at the risk of her own life, later married Salmon, a nobleman from the tribe of Judah. From her line of descendants came King David. Rahab was saved and blessed because she had faith in the God of Israel.

CHOOSE THIS DAY
Joshua 23-24

Joshua lived to be more than 100. When he knew he would soon die, he called his people together to give his last words. The elders and rulers and judges of the tribes met him at Shechem, in the middle of the land near his home. There Joshua reminded them of all God had done for their fathers and for them. He spoke of Abraham leaving his home at God's call. Of Jacob and his family going down to Egypt and, many years later, God bringing them out of that land. Of the Lord leading the Israelites through the wilderness and giving them the land where they now lived in peace.

"You are living in cities you did not build," the faithful old leader said. "You eat of vines and olive trees you did not plant. The Lord has given you all these things. Fear the Lord and serve Him with all your hearts.

"If any of you have any other gods, put them away. Serve the Lord only. If you are not willing to serve the Lord, you must choose this day the god you will serve." He straightened his shoulders. His eyes flashed with the old fire and dedication. "As for me and my house, we will serve the Lord!" His voice rang.

The people cried, "We will not turn away from the Lord to serve other gods! We will serve the Lord, for He is the God of Israel."

"Remember the Lord is strict in His commands," Joshua warned. "He will be angry if you turn away from Him after promising to serve Him. He will punish you if you worship images, as do the people around you."

The people vowed, "We pledge ourselves to serve the Lord and Him only."

Joshua wrote their promise in the book of the law, so others might read it and remember. He set up a great stone under an oak tree in Shechem. "Let this stone stand as a witness between you and the Lord, that you have pledged yourselves to be faithful to Him."

Joshua sent the people away to their own lands, having done all he could for them and telling them never to forget their promise. He died at 110, but as long as people lived who remembered Joshua, Israel continued serving the Lord.

DEBORAH
Judges 4-5

T he only woman judge ever to rule the Israelites was Deborah. She sat under a palm tree north of Jerusalem and gave advice to all those who approached her. She was so wise and good, people respected her judgment and brought all kinds of disputes. Deborah ruled because God's Spirit helped her.

When she heard that Jabin, a Canaanite king, had sent many iron chariots drawn by horses to attack the Israelites, she sent for a strong man named Barak.

"Call out those tribes of Israel who live near to you. The Lord has told me he will give the Canaanite army to you."

Barak told her, "If you will go with me, I will go. Otherwise, I will not."

"Because you did not trust God and go when He called you, the honor of winning shall not be yours," Deborah told Barak. She and Barak gathered an army of 10,000 men, who gathered on Mount Tabor. They attacked the Canaanites so suddenly, the enemy had no time to prepare. The soldiers ran away, trampled one another underfoot: chariots, horses, and men were all in wild flight. After the battle, peace lasted for many years.

GIDEON
Judges 6-7

O ne would think, after all God did for the Israelites, they would keep their promise to serve Him. They did not. When things went well, the very people God had delivered forgot the Lord and began to worship false gods like Baal and Asherah.

This worship of idols displeased God. He allowed some of the twelve tribes to be attacked, especially the tribes of Ephraim and Manasseh. For seven years the Midianites (Arabs) swept over their land at harvest-time, carrying away crops so the Israelites had no food for themselves or their sheep and cattle. They had to take refuge in mountain caves, leaving their villages and farms.

One day a man named Gideon was threshing wheat in a hidden place. He saw an angel sitting under an oak tree. "You are brave, Gideon," the angel said. "Go out and save your people from the Midianites."

"How can I save Israel?" Gideon cried. "I am of a poor family, the youngest in my father's house."

"I will be with you and help you drive out the Midianites," the promise came.

Gideon felt the angel was really the Lord. He brought an offering and laid it on a rock. The angel touched it with his staff. Fire leaped up and burned it, which made Gideon afraid, but the Lord said, "Peace be unto you, Gideon. Do not fear, for I am with you."

That night Gideon and ten men went to the house of Gideon's father. They tore down the images of two false gods, Baal and Asherah. In their places, Gideon erected an altar to the God of Israel, laid on the broken pieces of the idol Baal, and offered a young ox to God.

The next morning the people saw what Gideon had done and threatened to kill him. His father said, "If Baal is a god, he can take care of himself and punish the man who destroyed his image." When they saw that Baal could not harm Gideon, the people turned back to their own Lord God.

Gideon wanted to be very sure God was leading him

against the Midianites. He prayed, "Lord God, give me some sign that You will save Israel through me. Here is a fleece of wool (sheepskin). If tomorrow morning, the fleece is wet with dew and the grass around it dry, I will know you are with me and will give me victory over the Midianites."

What Gideon asked came to pass. He found the fleece soaked with dew, lying on dry grass. Still he had to be sure. "Lord, don't be angry with me. Please, give me one more sign. Tomorrow morning, let the fleece be dry and the ground wet with dew and I will doubt no more." This also happened. Gideon went forth to meet the enemy. God directed him every step of the way and brought victory.

SAMSON
Judges 13-16

S amson, son of Manoah, was the strongest man in the Bible. Before Samson was born, an angel came to Manoah's wife and told her, "You shall have a son who will begin to save Israel from the Philistines. He must never drink any wine or strong drink as long as he lives. His hair must grow long and never be cut, for he shall be a Nazarite, under a vow to the Lord."

Samson was so strong as a young man that he easily killed a lion that roared down the mountainside. Samson also did many other things, including killing almost a thousand Philistines with only the jawbone of an ass for a weapon. Then he fell in love with Delilah, a Philistine woman who did not worship the Lord God. She teased and teased to learn the secret of Samson's strength. At last he told her, "I am under a vow to the Lord never to drink wine or allow my hair to be cut. I believe if I did, the Lord would forsake me and with Him would go my strength."

While Samson slept with his head on treacherous Delilah's knees, rulers of the Philistines shaved off all his hair. Delilah called, "Rise up, Samson! The Philistines are after you!"

Samson rose, but his strength had gone. The Philistines took him prisoner, blinded and chained him and sent him to prison at Gaza. There he had to turn a heavy millstone to grind grain, as though he were an animal. In prison, his hair grew long again.

One day the Philistines made a great feast in the temple of their fish-god Dagon. They brought Samson out to taunt him. Thousands of people jeered at him. Samson asked the boy who led him to take him where he might stand between two pillars and lean against them. When he got there he prayed, "Lord, God, remember me! Give me strength once more, to obtain vengeance on the Philistines for my two eyes." He placed arms around the pillars on either side, pulled them over and brought down the roof, killing more Philistines in his death than he had killed during his life.

RUTH AND NAOMI
Book of Ruth

Elimelech, his wife Naomi, and their two sons Mahlon and Chilion lived in Bethlehem, about six miles south of Jerusalem. Year after year the crops grew less until famine threatened. At last, Elimelech reluctantly took his family to the land of Moab. They stayed there ten years. During that time, Elimelech died. So did his sons, but not before they had married Moabite women.

Orpah and Ruth clung to their mother-in-law Naomi. When she heard God had again given good harvest and bread to the land of Judah, she decided to go back to Bethlehem. She told her daughters-in-law, "Go back to your mothers' homes. May the Lord deal kindly with you, as you have been kind to your husbands and me. May He grant that you each find another husband and a happy home." She kissed them farewell.

"You have been a good mother to us," the girls cried. "We will go and live with you among your people."

"No, no," Naomi protested. "You are young and I am old. I have no more sons to be your husbands."

Orpah tearfully returned to her people but Ruth would not leave Naomi. She quietly said, "Do not ask me to leave you. I never will. Where you go, I will go. Where you live, I will live. Your people shall be my people, and your God shall be my God. Where you die, I will die and be buried. Nothing but death can ever part us."

So Naomi stopped trying to persuade Ruth to go back, and the two walked around the Dead Sea, crossed the river Jordan, climbed the mountains of Judah, and came to Bethlehem. Naomi's friends were glad to see her, but she said, "Do not call me Naomi, which means pleasant. I come home empty, without husband or sons. Call me Mara, which means 'Bitter.'"

The two women settled down in Bethlehem. Naomi sent Ruth to glean. She gathered stalks at harvest time left for the poor people by the owners of the fields. Ruth gleaned in the fields of Boaz, a rich man related to Elimelech. Boaz saw Ruth gleaning in his fields and inquired about her.

"She is the young woman Naomi brought from Moab," his reapers said.

"Daughter, do not go to any other field. Stay in my fields with my young women and no one shall harm you. When you are thirsty, go drink from our water jugs."

Ruth bowed, thanked him, and later joyfully reported the conversation to Naomi. Boaz also said, "I have heard how true you are to your mother-in-law. May the Lord, under whose wings you have come from your own land, give you a reward." At midday, he gave her food, then privately told his reapers to drop extra sheaves so Ruth might gather them.

Naomi's heart lifted when she heard of Boaz's kindness. She advised Ruth to do as he said and stay in his fields only. Ruth did. When the harvest ended, she and Boaz fell in love. Naomi lived with them after the marriage and was no longer bitter.

Ruth, the young woman of Moab who chose the people and God of Israel, became the mother of kings. She and Boaz had a son named Obed. He grew up, married, and had a son called Jesse. Jesse was the father of David, the shepherd boy who became a king.

YOUNG SAMUEL
1 Samuel 1-3

Hannah, wife of Elkanah, grieved over her lack of children. On one of their yearly visits to the house of the Lord in Shiloh, she prayed earnestly. "O Lord, if You will give me a son, he shall be given to the Lord as long as he lives."

The Lord heard Hannah's prayer and gave her a son. She named him Samuel, which means "asked of God." While he was still a small child, Hannah kept her vow and brought him to the priest Eli. She brokenly said, "I asked God for this child and promised he would be the Lord's as long as he lives. Let Samuel stay here with you and grow up in God's house."

Young Samuel lived with Eli in a tent beside the Tabernacle at Shiloh. He helped the priest in the work of the Lord's house. He was a comfort to Eli, for the priest's own sons were wicked and almost broke their father's heart. The old man prayed and prayed for them, but could do nothing to stop their sinful ways.

One night Samuel lay on his bed. He heard a voice call "Samuel."

The young boy jumped from his bed and ran to Eli. "Here I am. What do you want me to do?"

"I did not call you," Eli told him. "Go and lie down again."

Samuel obeyed, but soon the voice called again. "Samuel."

For the second time the child ran to Eli, but the old man told him he had not called and sent him back to his bed.

The third time the voice called and the boy came to Eli, the priest realized it was the voice of the Lord. He said, "Go lie down once more. If the voice calls again, say 'Speak, Lord, for thy servant heareth.'"

Samuel did as he was told. The Lord said, "I have seen the wickedness of Eli's sons. And I have seen that their father did not punish them for doing evil. Now I will punish them in such a way the story will make everyone's ears tingle."

Samuel lay on his bed until morning, then went about his work, saying nothing of God's voice until Eli asked. When he hesitantly repeated the Lord's message, Eli sadly bowed his head. "It is the Lord," the old priest said. "Let Him do what seems good to Him."

The news went throughout all the land that God had

again spoken to His people. Hannah, the lonely mother, heard that God had chosen her son to be His prophet and speak with Him. From that time on, God spoke to Samuel and the boy gave God's word to the twelve tribes of Israel.

THE ARK IS CAPTURED
1 Samuel 4-7

Badly beaten by the Philistines, the Israelite chiefs made a bold move. They took the Ark of the Covenant from the Tabernacle into battle, believing the Lord would be with them. The wicked sons of Eli went to care for the ark.

On the day of the battle, Eli, old and blind, sat beside the door of the Tabernacle, heart trembling for the ark of the Lord. A man came running from the army, garments torn and earth on his head as a sign of sorrow. "There has been a terrible battle," he gasped. "The Philistines have killed thousands of our people. Your sons are dead." The man shook with fright. "The enemy has taken the ark of God into their own land!"

The shock was so great, Eli fell backward from his seat, broke his neck, and died.

The Philistines put the ark of God in the temple of the fish-headed idol Dagon in one of their chief cities. The next morning, Dagon's image lay on its face before the ark of the Lord. They stood it up, but on the next morning it lay bowed down again. This time the hands and head of Dagon had been cut off and also lay on the floor.

Fear swept through the people. So did boils and sores. They saw the hand of God in all this and sent the ark to another city. Those people were also afflicted with boils and sores. They cried, "We will not have the ark among us. Send it back to its own land or surely we will all die."

For twenty years, the ark stood in the house of a man named Abinadab in Kirjath-jearim. They did not take it back to Shiloh. After Eli's death, the Tabernacle fell into ruins and no one lived there again.

GOD KEEPS HIS PROMISE
1 Samuel 7

When Samuel grew up, he went among the tribes and told the people what God wanted them to know. "If you will repent and come back with all your heart to the Lord God of Israel; if you will put away false gods and seek the Lord, then God will set you free from the Philistines."

People began to throw down the idols and pray to God. Samuel prayed for them and they confessed their wrongdoing and solemnly promised to serve Him. The Philistines came against them with sword and spear. This frightened the Israelites. They had not fought the Philistines for more than twenty years and had no weapons or training.

Samuel offered a lamb to the Lord and prayed mightily for God to help Israel.

God heard and answered. A great storm came, rare in that area. Thunder boomed and lightning flashed so heavily it frightened the Philistines. They threw down their spears and ran away.

For the rest of the time Samuel ruled as judge over Israel and taught the people to worship the Lord God, peace reigned throughout the land.

KING SAUL
1 Samuel 8-15

When Samuel grew old, the people demanded that he find a king for them. Samuel asked God what to do, for he knew it was wrong. God said, "They have turned away from me in asking for a king. Let them have one, but show them the wrong they are doing and the trouble their king will bring to them."

Samuel obeyed. He told the elders of the people, "A king will take your sons and make some of them soldiers, horsemen, men to drive his chariots. He will take other sons to wait on him, work in his fields, and make his chariots and weapons of war. Your king will take your best fields and farms and give them to men of his court. He will make your daughters cook and bake and serve in his palace. He will take some of your animals. He will be your master and make you his servants."

The people still cried for a king, someone to lead them in war. God wanted the Israelites to be quiet and plain and live apart, serving Him. They wanted to be great and strong in war, and have riches and power. The Lord said to Samuel, "Do as they ask. Choose them a king."

After a time, a large good-looking young man named Saul came to Samuel. God told His prophet Saul would rule over the people. Samuel poured oil on the young man's head, saying, "The Lord has anointed you to be prince over His land and His people." He gave Saul instructions and promised that the Lord would give the noble young man His Spirit and a new heart to show that God was with Saul.

Samuel assembled the people at Mizpah. He announced Saul was now their king. After 300 years under fifteen judges, Israel had a king. Some were not pleased. They asked, "Can such a man as *this* save us?" Saul ignored them.

At first Saul lived at home and worked his fields just as he had always done, even though he was king. Then the Ammonites, a fierce people from the desert beyond the Jordan, attacked. Saul gathered a great army and won the battle. He and Samuel offered sacrifices to the Lord and worshipped.

Samuel reminded the people God had given them a king. He said, "If you fear the Lord and serve Him, things will go well. If you disobey the Lord, God will punish you as He punished your fathers." He bid them farewell, left Saul in charge, and went back to his house at Ramah.

Two years after Saul became king, he did a terrible thing. Samuel had warned Saul not to march against the Philistines until he came to offer sacrifices to the Lord. Saul did not wait for Samuel, but offered a sacrifice himself.

"What have you done?" Samuel demanded when he came.

"I saw that my men were scattering. I feared the enemy might attack, so I offered the sacrifice, since you were not here," Saul confessed.

"You have done wrong." Samuel told him. "God would have kept you safe if you had obeyed. Now He will find another man to do His will—a man after His own heart. Someday God will take the kingdom from you and give it to him."

In spite of the warning, Saul led 600 men against the Philistines. Just before the battle, he commanded the men not to eat until sundown, lest they die. Saul's son Jonathan had not heard the command. He ate honey and grew stronger because of it. Saul intended to kill Jonathan for innocently breaking his command, but the people rescued and freed him.

Although a great victory had been won over the

enemy, Saul had already proved himself unfit to rule. He acted too hastily and did not obey God's commands. Time after time, Saul choose his way instead of God's. Samuel prayed all night and went to meet Saul. The king insisted that he had obeyed God, but he did not fool Samuel, for the Lord had told him differently. Again Samuel warned, "Saul, God will give the kingdom to a better man." He went away and never saw Saul again, but he mourned and wept for the man who disobeyed and was rejected as a king by the Lord.

DAVID AND GOLIATH
1 Samuel 16-17

The Lord led Samuel to a man named Jesse and directed him to anoint the youngest son, a shepherd boy named David. From that day, the Spirit of the Lord was with David. He grew up strong and brave, fighting off bears and lions that tried to harm his flock. God talked with David and showed him His will.

The Spirit of God left King Saul because of his disobedience. Saul became gloomy, only rousing to cheerfulness when someone played the harp. He learned that David of Bethlehem played well and sent for him. Saul loved David, as everyone else did, for the Lord was with him. He soothed away Saul's troubles with his harp, and the king made him armor bearer. David carried his shield, spear, and sword, but Saul did not know that Samuel had anointed the lad to be king.

War continued. One day a giant came from the Philistine camp, daring someone to come fight him. Goliath stood nine feet tall and wore armor from head to foot. No man in the army, not even King Saul, dared fight him. David said, "If no one else will go, I will fight this enemy of the Lord's people."

King Saul raised his eyebrows. "You are not able to fight the giant. You are too young."

"I have fought lions and bears," David said. "I am not afraid."

Saul put his own armor on David, but it didn't fit at all, so David refused it. "Let me fight my own way," he said. He took his shepherd's staff in his hand, as though it were his weapon. He also carried a slingshot and five smooth stones in a little bag as he trotted out to meet the giant.

"Am I a dog that this boy comes to me with a stick?" Goliath jeered.

David answered, "You come against me with a sword, a spear, and a dart. I come to you in the name of the Lord of hosts, the God of the armies of Israel. This day the Lord will give you into my hand that all may know there is a God in Israel." Then David ran toward Goliath, took out his sling, and hurled a stone at the giant's forehead. It stunned Goliath, and he fell to the ground. Before he could rise, David ran forward, drew out the giant's sword, and used it to kill Goliath!

When the Philistines knew their great warrior was dead, they turned to run toward their own land. The Israelites followed and won a mighty victory.

SAUL AND DAVID
1 Samuel 17-31

S aul has slain his thousands, and David his ten thousands," the people cried.

This made Saul angry and jealous. He hated

David, but dared not kill him. He sent David on many dangerous errands of war, but the Lord always saved him. Saul's son Jonathan loved David. He helped deliver him from his father's schemes and David hid in the mountains. At one time, David spared Saul's life. He would not harm the man God had anointed as king.

Time passed. The prophet Samuel had died years before. Saul was old and weak. He heard of a woman known as the Witch of Endor who could call up spirits of the dead. He was so anxious to have some message from the Lord, he dressed as a common man and came to her. Through the witch Saul spoke to the spirit of Samuel. "I am in great distress," he pleaded. "Tell me what to do. God has forsaken me."

"If the Lord has forsaken you, why call on me?" the spirit of Samuel replied. "Tomorrow the Lord will give Israel to the Philistines. You and your sons shall be dead."

It came to pass. Three of Saul's sons, including brave and noble Jonathan, died in battle. Saul killed himself with his own sword.

DAVID THE KING
Book of 2 Samuel

David became king at age 37. He reigned over all Israel for 33 years. As long as he served the Lord, he prospered. David prepared a new Tabernacle on Mount Zion and brought the Ark of the covenant from its hiding place. He fought many wars and at last saw peace again come to the land.

One evening at sunset he looked down from the roof of his palace and saw a beautiful woman. He desired her, but could not marry Bathsheba while her husband Uriah was living. David did a wicked thing. He sent Uriah into the middle of battle so he would be killed. Few knew what had happened when Uriah was killed in battle, but God knew and was displeased. He sent Nathan the prophet to tell David he must pay for his sin. "You shall suffer," Nathan said. "So will all your family."

David felt such sorrow for sinning against the Lord God forgave him. David's first child by Bathsheba died. She had another son, Solomon, who grew up to be a wise man. Most of David's sons were wicked; chief among them was Absalom, whom David loved more than any other son. Absalom had long hair, of which he was very proud. He was said to be the most beautiful young man in all the land. His heart, however, did not match his beauty. He killed his own brother Amnon, fled, and didn't return to the palace for three years. Then he set himself up as king. David escaped with Bathsheba, little Solomon, and a few others.

Absalom's rule didn't last. Fleeing into a wood from a battle, his long hair caught in a tree's branches, where he was left hanging and later killed. His father grieved, saying, "My son, my son Absalom! I wish I had died for you!"

David ruled for many years more, through good times and bad. He saw angels, witnessed pestilence, repented for his wickedness, and received God's forgiveness. He stored up many precious things for the Temple to be built on Mount Moriah, although he knew, it would not be built by him. "You have been a man of war and shed much blood," God said, "My house shall be built by a man of peace. When you die, your son Solomon shall reign. He shall have a peaceful reign, and he shall build My temple."

DAVID CHOOSES A KING
1 Kings 1-2

Davrid grew old and was ready to turn the throne over to his son Solomon. However, he had great opposition from his older sons, especially Adonijah, who decided to be king. He met with the general of the army and a high priest outside the city wall. There they had a great feast and prepared to crown Adonijah.

David had become feeble and no longer went out of the palace, but he had not lost his wisdom. He heard of Adonijah's plot and said, "Let us make Solomon king at once and put an end to the plans of these men." He commanded his servants to bring forth the mule on which no one but the king was allowed to ride. They placed Solomon on the animal's back. With the king's guard, nobles, and great men, they brought Solomon down to the valley south of the city.

Zadok the priest took the horn filled with holy oil used for anointing the priests to set them apart for their work. He poured oil on Solomon's head. The priests blew the trumpets and all the people cried, "God save King Solomon!"

Adonijah and his friends heard the trumpets and shouting. "What is the cause of all this noise and uproar?" they wanted to know.

Just then a messenger raced to them. "King David has made Solomon king.

"David sent a message saying, 'Blessed be the Lord, who has given me a son to sit on my throne!'"

Fear filled Adonijah and his friends. He ran to the altar of the Lord and knelt in the holy place, hoping Solomon would have mercy on him.

Solomon said, "If Adonijah will do right and be true

to me, no harm shall come to him." His brother came and bowed down before King Solomon. He promised to be true to him and was allowed to go home.

Not long afterwards, David summoned Solomon to his bedside. He gave his last advice to the new king; then he died, having reigned forty years. They buried David on Mount Zion, where his tomb remained standing for many years.

SOLOMON'S WISDOM
1 Kings 3; 2 Chronicles 1

Great responsibility lay on the young man, scarcely more than a boy, who had ascended to the throne. Not more than twenty, Solomon now ruled the kingdom of Israel at the peak of its growth.

Soon after he became king, Solomon went to Gibeon, a few miles north of Jerusalem, where the altar of the Lord stood before the Temple was built. He made offerings and worshiped the Lord God of Israel.

That night God came to him and said, "Ask whatever you choose and I will give it to you."

Solomon said, "Lord, I am only a child. I don't know how to rule this great people. Give me wisdom and knowledge, that I may rule them well."

This pleased the Lord. He told Solomon, "You have not asked for long life or great riches. You do not seek victory over your enemies or great power. Instead, you ask for wisdom and knowledge to judge this people. I have given you wisdom greater than any king before you or any who will come after you. Because you have asked this, I will give you not only your wisdom, but all honor and riches.

If you obey my words as your father David obeyed, you shall have a long life and rule for many years."

Soon after this, Solomon's wisdom was put to the test. Two women came to him with babies, one dead, the other living. Each said the living child was hers. One complained, "We were sleeping with our children in one bed. This woman in her sleep lay on her child and it died. She put it beside me while I slept and took my baby. In the morning she claimed my child as hers."

The other woman said it was not true, but a trick to get her child.

Solomon considered the problem then said to a guard, "Take a sword, divide the living child and give half to each woman."

One cried out, "No, do not kill my child! Give the baby to her, but let it live."

The other woman said, "Cut the child in two and divide it between us."

Solomon sternly said, "Give the child to the woman who would not have it slain. She is the real mother." All the people marveled at Solomon's wisdom.

SOLOMON'S TEMPLE
1 Kings 5-6; 2 Chronicles 3

Solomon's great work was building the Temple. The house of God covered the whole mountain called Mount Moriah. David had prepared for it by gathering great stores of gold, silver, stone, and wood. King Hiram of Tyre on the seacoast, friend of Solomon, had his men cut cedar trees on Mount Lebanon. From Tyre, they were floated down to Joppa, then taken ashore and carried up to Jerusalem.

The Temple was copied after the Tabernacle, except it was much larger. The stone walls and the cedar roof replaced the earlier tent materials. Seven long years men sweated and labored before the Temple was completed and dedicated to the Lord. When the sun struck the walls, they dazzled those who came to worship.

One night the Lord appeared to Solomon. "I have heard your prayers and made this house holy," He said. "It shall be My house and I will dwell there." God reminded Solomon to walk before Him as had David, his father. He promised, "If you do this, your throne shall stand forever. If you turn aside from following the Lord, I will leave this house. I will turn from it and let the enemies of Israel come and destroy this house that was built for Me."

THE QUEEN OF SHEBA
1 Kings 10

Solomon's fame spread far beyond the borders of the countries he ruled. Many nations sent princes to visit him. All wondered at his skill in answering hard questions and called King Solomon the wisest man in the world. He wrote many of the sayings in the Book of Proverbs and more than a thousand songs. People came both to see Solomon's riches and to hear his wise words.

The Queen of Sheba lived in southern Arabia, more than a thousand miles from Jerusalem. All this talk of Solomon's wisdom intrigued her and made her curious. She and her company of nobles rode camels, brought lavish gifts, and came to visit King Solomon. She received a royal welcome, as befitted her station in life, then asked hard questions designed to test the King's ability. To her amazement, he answered every one! He showed her the glory of his palace: his throne and his servants, the richness of his table, the steps from his palace to the house of the Lord.

The Queen looked and listened. Then she said, "All I heard of your wisdom and greatness is true. I did not believe it until I came and saw your kingdom. Not half was told me. Your wisdom and splendor are far greater than I heard. Happy are those who hear your wisdom! Blessed be the Lord, your God, who has set you on the throne of Israel!" She gave Solomon treasures of gold, sweet-smelling spices and perfumes. Solomon also gave her rich presents. Then the Queen of Sheba began the long journey back to her own land.

SOLOMON'S PUNISHMENT
1 Kings 11

O would think Solomon with all his blessings would cling close to the Lord, appreciating what he had been given. He did for a time, but his palaces and walled cities, splendid court, and entertaining cost money. He taxed the people heavily to help pay for them. He compelled many to work on his buildings, become soldiers in his army, labor in his fields, and serve in his household. He did all the things Samuel had warned the people would happen when they asked for a king against the Lord's will. Before Solomon's reign ended, the people cried out against him for the heavy burdens he laid on the land.

Wise in the affairs of the world, Solomon neither cared about the poor nor loved God with all his heart. He married a daughter of Pharaoh of Egypt, made her queen and built her a costly palace. He also married many other kings' daughters. Worse, Solomon built a temple of idols on the Mount of Olives. The idols stood on the hill in front of Jerusalem and even the king offered sacrifices to these images!

This idol worship made the Lord very angry. He said, "You have done wicked things. You have not kept your promise to serve Me. You have ignored my commands. Because of this, I will take away the kingdom of Israel from your son and give it to one of your servants. But for the sake of your father David, who loved and obeyed me, I will not take away all the kingdom, but will leave him and his children one tribe."

The servant God chose was an able man named Jeroboam, of the tribe of Ephraim. One day Ahijah, a prophet of the Lord, met Jeroboam as he was going out of Jerusalem. Ahijah took off his cloak and tore it into twelve pieces. He gave ten to Jeroboam, promising him God would tear ten tribes out of the hand of Solomon's son and give them to Jeroboam.

King Solomon heard about what the prophet had said. He sent men to kill Jeroboam, but the man who would one day be king fled to Egypt and stayed there until Solomon died. Solomon reigned forty years, as had David. Solomon's son Rehoboam followed him as king.

Sometimes the reign of Solomon has been called "the Golden Age of Israel" because of its peace and riches. Better to call it the "Gilded Age." Beneath the show and glitter of Solomon's reign lay oppression and many evil things.

JEROBOAM AND REHOBOAM
1 Kings 12-14

After Solomon died, the people rose up against his weak son Rehoboam. The strongest (and most foolish) thing Rehoboam did was refuse to listen to the people who advised that he lift their heavy burdens. Ten of the tribes broke away from Rehoboam's rule and the house of David. They made Jeroboam their king. This broke up the empire of Solomon. All this was the will of the Lord. He wished Israel to become a good people, not a great nation; to live for Him, not for the world.

Jeroboam could have been a great king. His descendants might have ruled for a long time. All he had to do was serve the Lord. He did not. Instead of trusting the Lord, he took matters into his own hands, set up a calf of gold at places of worship he made at Bethel in the south and Dan in the north.

"It is too far for you to go to Jerusalem," he told the people. "Here are gods for you, gods that brought you out of Egypt. Come and worship them."

The priests of Levi would not serve in Jeroboam's idol temples, so he took men out of all the tribes and made them priests. He set up more images in the land to lead the people into worshipping idols.

Every fall the people went to a feast in Jerusalem. Jeroboam made a feast at Bethel to draw them away from the Temple of the Lord at Jerusalem. For this reason, the Bible calls him, "Jeroboam, who made Israel to sin."

One day while Jeroboam was offering incense at the altar, a prophet from Judah came and cried out against the altar. "Thus saith the Lord: 'Behold, in the time to come there shall rise up a man of the house of David, Josiah by name. He shall burn upon this altar the bones of the priests who sacrifice to idols in this place. This altar and this temple shall be destroyed.'"

The prophet told Jeroboam, "I will prove I am speaking for God. This altar shall fall apart and the ashes on it shall be poured out."

King Jeroboam grew angry. He stretched out his hand toward the prophet and called to his guards, "Seize this man!" Instantly Jeroboam's outstretched hand dried up and became helpless. The altar crumbled and the ashes poured onto the ground. Jeroboam knew then this was the work of the Lord. He pleaded with the prophet to call on God, so He would make the afflicted hand well. The prophet prayed. God healed Jeroboam's hand, but the prophet would neither eat nor drink. He went home to Judah by another way.

Because King Jeroboam led the people into sin, the kingdom was taken away from his family and they all perished.

ELIJAH AND THE WIDOW
1 Kings 17

During the reign of Ahab, a king worse than any before him, his wife Jezebel hated the prophets of the Lord. Because he sought them out and had them killed, many hid in caves in the mountains.

A new prophet suddenly appeared. Elijah wore rough, skin clothing and had long hair and a beard. He lived alone in the wilderness. During a time of famine, at God's command, ravens brought Elijah food and he drank from a brook until it dried up. Then the prophet followed God's instructions and went to Zarephath.

Elijah met a woman at the well. She brought him water, as he asked. When he said, "Bring me a little piece of bread," she looked sad.

"I only have a handful of meal in the barrel and a few drops of oil in a bottle. I am gathering sticks to make a fire and bake a little cake for me and my son. When we have eaten it, there is nothing left for us to do but die."

The word of the Lord came to Elijah. He told the woman, "Fear not. Go do as you have said but first make me a little cake, then cook for yourself and your son. God says you will have grain and oil until the rains come."

The widow believed Elijah. She made the cake and found enough meal and oil left to feed herself and her son. As long as the prophet, the widow, and her boy needed it, meal and oil remained in barrel and bottle.

One day the lad fell ill. Elijah cried to God on his behalf. He stretched himself over the child's body three times, asking the Lord to let the child's soul come into him again. The Lord heard his servant's prayer and the child came alive. Elijah carried the lad back to his mother and she said, "Now I am sure you are a man of God. The word of the Lord you speak is truth."

ELIJAH'S WORK
1 Kings 18-19; 2 Kings 1

Ahab worshipped Jezebel's wicked gods Baal and Asherah. Still he sought out Elijah to call down rain on the parched land. Elijah challenged the false prophets to pit their power against the Lord. Hundreds of people gathered on Mount Carmel. Elijah told the people, "Today you will see who is the true God. Stop your uncertainty. Either choose the Lord God of Israel, or Baal."

The priests placed an oxen sacrifice on the altar of Baal, but did not light the wood beneath it. Elijah had said surely a true god would send fire. The priests cried, "Hear us, O Baal!" Nothing happened. They called again. Still nothing happened. It enraged them.

Elijah hugely enjoyed the spectacle. "Call louder," he told them. "Perhaps your god is thinking or gone on a journey. He may be sleeping. Awaken him!"

By mid-afternoon, there was no more sign of fire on the altar of Baal than there had been when the people gathered around it hours earlier. Murmurings in the multitude increased.

Now came Elijah's turn. He found an altar to the Lord that had been thrown down. He piled up twelve stones, one for each tribe of Israel, dug a trench to carry away water. He stacked wood, placed on it the oxen sacrifice, then drenched it with so many barrels of water even the trench filled. Next, Elijah prayed for God to send fire.

Fire fell from the sky. It burned up the offering, wood, stones, and dust. It even licked up the water in the trench! The multitude fell on their faces crying, "The Lord is God!" Elijah commanded that the prophets of Baal be seized and killed for leading Israel into sin. He prayed mightily and rain poured from a small cloud that rose from the sea. That day people turned away from the defeated Baal and to the true God.

This incident made Jezebel hate Elijah more than ever. Elijah ran for his life. Tired, hungry and discouraged, he no longer wanted to live. He fell asleep under a juniper tree on the burning sand. When he awakened, he saw a fire with a loaf of bread baking on it and a bottle of water.

Later God sent Elijah to stand on the mountain. A great wind swept by and broke the rocks in pieces, but

the Lord was not in the wind. An earthquake shook
the mountain, but the Lord was not in the earthquake. A
fire passed by, but the Lord was not in the fire. Then
came silence. In the stillness, Elijah heard a low, quiet
voice he knew was the Lord's. God sent him back to
anoint some new kings and a young man named Elisha to
take Elijah's place as a prophet.

God's intervention gave Elijah what he needed most:
work, a friend, and the knowledge that seven thousand
faithful men still lived in Israel. He faithfully served God
until the Lord sent a chariot and horses of fire to take
Elijah to heaven in a whirlwind. Elisha took up Elijah's
work and did many wonderful things for the Lord and
His people.

NAAMAN, THE LEPER
2 Kings 5

Naaman, general of the Syrian army, was brave and
great in rank and power. Imagine his feelings
when he discovered he had leprosy! In those days, lepers
always died. An Israelite girl who served in Naaman's
home, told Naaman's wife of the prophet Elisha. "He
could cure the leprosy," she said. So Naaman went seeking Elisha.

To his dismay, Elisha didn't even come out of his
house. He sent his servant to tell Naaman, "Go wash
seven times in the river Jordan and you will be well."

Naaman grew angry at this command, but his servants coaxed him to do what the prophet said. Naaman
did and his leprous skin became clean and healthy!

JONAH
Book of Jonah

The prophet Jonah was always getting into trouble. First he didn't want to preach to the sinners in Nineveh when God told him to do this. He got on a ship and headed as far in the other direction as possible. The Lord caused a great storm to come on the sea. The sailors threw everything they could overboard. They cast lots to see whose fault it was. When they learned Jonah was running away from God, they rowed hard to bring the ship to land, then reluctantly cast Jonah into the raging sea.

The storm ceased, but God had prepared a great fish that swallowed Jonah. For three miserable days Jonah lived inside the fish, a prophecy of the days between Christ's burial and resurrection. He prayed and prayed. At last the Lord made the big fish spit Jonah out onto dry land.

Again God told him to go to Nineveh. This time Jonah went. He told the people, "Within forty days, Nineveh will be destroyed!" The people believed him. They turned from their sins, fasted, and prayed to the Lord. God forgave them and spared their city.

Jonah got angry. It made him look like a false prophet. Besides, these people were his enemies. He built a hut and sat under a gourd plant that shaded him; while he pouted and sulked, a worm destroyed the plant. Then a hot wind blew. God told Jonah if he could have pity on a plant, should not God have pity on a city with more than 100,000 little children?

Jonah at last learned that even people who don't know God are precious to Him and loved by Him.

THE TEMPLE RESTORED
2 Chronicles 24

King Joash wanted the Temple of the Lord made new and beautiful. It had grown old and decayed since Solomon built it. Those who followed Baal broke down the walls and carried away the gold and silver to use in their worship.

The king placed a large box at the door so everyone would see it when they went to worship the Lord. The box had a hole in the lid. The king sent word throughout the land that the princes and people should bring money and drop it into the chest whenever they came to the Temple.

Those who came gladly brought their gifts, for they wanted God's house to once again be beautiful. In a short time, gold and silver filled the box. The king's officers opened the chest, tied up the money in bags and put it away for safekeeping. They did this again and again until they had enough money to pay for repairing the Temple and for making new ornaments of gold and silver.

After the good priest Jehoiada died, King Joash had no one to teach him the proper way to act. The princes who loved to worship idols led the king astray, after he had done so much good! God was not pleased when Joash abandoned Him. He allowed the Syrians from the north to attack. They robbed the cities and left Joash sick and poor. Soon afterwards, his own servants killed him and made his son Amaziah king in his place.

MANY KINGS
2 Chronicles 22-28

So many kings came and went to the thrones of Judah and Israel, it's a wonder the people could keep track of them! Many began their rule worshipping God. As long as they served Him, things went well. Yet too often the kings turned from the Lord God of Israel and went their own wicked ways. Many allowed themselves to be persuaded to worship Baal and other idols. When the prophets protested, the kings warned them to hold their tongues if they wished to live.

One king who did right in the sight of the Lord for most of the 52 years he reigned was Uzziah, tenth king of Judah. He was only 16 when crowned. The Lord helped him make the kingdom strong again and won back much land.

Sadly, when he grew strong and rich, his heart became proud. Uzziah wanted to have the power of the high priest as well as that of the king. He went into the Holy Place of the Temple to offer incense on the golden altar, although only priests were allowed to do this. The high priest Azariah and some other priests followed Uzziah into the Holy Place. He said, "It is not for you to be in the Holy Place or offer incense. This belongs to the priests alone. Go out! You have disobeyed the Lord's command. It will bring you trouble, not honor."

Uzziah stood before the golden altar with a censer of incense in his hand. White scales of leprosy instantly rose on his forehead. Uzziah turned to leave. The priests would not wait but drove him out. Uzziah remained a leper until he died. He could no longer sit as king, or live in the palace. When he died he was not buried in the tombs of the kings, but in a field outside.

Jotham, Uzziah's son, ruled next. He served the Lord but did nothing to stop his people from worshipping idols.

Ahaz became the twelfth and most wicked of all the kings of Judah. He not only worshipped the images of Baal, he sacrificed some of his own children as offerings to the false gods! In his reign, the house of the Lord was shut up and left to ruin; its treasures taken away. God brought great suffering to the land because of Ahaz and his people's wickedness. Assyrians later robbed Ahaz of all he had and laid heavy burdens on the people they ruled. When Ahaz died, he left his people worshippers of idols and under the power of the king of Assyria.

ISAIAH'S VISION
Isaiah 6

In the days of Uzziah, Jothan, and Ahaz, God raised up a great prophet in Judah to warn the people. The prophecies he spoke in the name of the Lord are given in the book named for him: Isaiah.

Isaiah was only a young man in the year King Uzziah died. One day while worshipping in the Temple, a wonderful vision came to him. He saw the Lord God on a throne, with the angels around him. He also saw strange creatures called seraphim standing before the throne of God. Each had six wings. Two covered the seraphims' faces before the glory of the Lord. Two covered their feet. They flew through the air with the other two, calling, "Holy, holy, is the Lord of hosts. The whole earth is full of His glory!"

Young Isaiah felt the Temple walls and floor shaking. A cloud of smoke covered the house and filled him with fear. He cried out, "Woe has come to me! I am a man of sinful lips and I live among a people of sinful lips. Now my eyes have seen the King, the Lord of hosts!"

One of the seraphim took the tongs used in the sacrifices. He flew to the altar and took a burning coal with the tongs then flew to Isaiah. He pressed the fiery coal to the young man's mouth and said, "This coal from God's altar has touched your lips. Your sin is taken away and you are made clean."

Isaiah heard God's voice say, "Whom shall I send to this people? Who will carry the message of the Lord to them?"

Isaiah replied, "Here I am, Lord. Send me."

"You shall be my prophet and go to this people and give them my word," the Lord told Isaiah. "They will not listen to you or understand. Your words will do them no good, but will seem to make their hearts hard, their ears heavy, and their eyes shut. They will not hear with their ears, or see with their eyes, or understand with their hearts, or turn to me and be saved."

Isaiah asked, "How long must this be, Lord?"

The Lord said, "Until the cities are left waste without people, the houses without men to live in them. The land shall become utterly desolate. The people shall be turned far away into another land. Out of this a few people a tenth will come back and rise like a new tree from the roots of the tree that was cut down. This tenth shall be the seed of a new people in times to come."

Isaiah felt reassured. Even though his words might seem to do no good, he must go on preaching. Long afterward, a new Judah would rise out of the kingdom and serve the Lord.

Isaiah lived for many years. He spoke the word of the Lord to his people until he was very old and preached while at least four kings ruled. Some were friendly and listened to him. Others would not obey the prophet and serve God. The kingdom of Judah gradually began worshipping idols instead of the Lord.

HEZEKIAH
2 Chronicles 29-32

After Ahaz, the worst king of Judah, came Hezekiah, the best. He listened to Isaiah and obeyed the Lord's commands. In the first month he reigned, Hezekiah called together the priests and Levites who had charge of the house of the Lord. "My sons," he said. "Give yourself again to the service of the Lord and be holy, as God commands you. Open the doors of His house that have been shut for years. Take away the idols. Clean and purify the Temple. We must return to the Lord and worship only Him."

They followed the Lord's commands. They also began keeping the Feast of the Passover that reminded the people how God had led the children of Israel out of Egypt. This Feast had not been observed for many years. King Hezekiah sent commands through all Judah for the people to come to Jerusalem and worship the Lord at this feast. He also sent men throughout Israel to ask the Ten Tribes to come up with their brothers in Judah to Jerusalem.

At that time, Hoshea, last king of Israel, sat on the throne of the Northern Kingdom. Overrun with Assyrians, the kingdom was weak and near its end. Most of the people had forgotten God's law and worshipped idols. They laughed at Hezekiah's messengers and would not come to the feast. But some in Israel had listened to the prophets. They came to worship with the men of Judah.

After the feast, King Hezekiah broke down images and destroyed idols. He tore down altars erected for worship of false gods and even cut down the trees under which the altars stood. Everywhere he called on his people to turn from their idols and worship the Lord God.

After a few years, Hezekiah felt strong enough to free Judah from Assyrian rule. He refused to pay tax, gathered an army, built the walls of Jerusalem higher and made ready for war. But Sennacherib, king of Assyria, came with a great army. He took the cities in the west of Judah and threatened to take Jerusalem.

Hezekiah saw he had made a mistake. He could not fight the Assyrians, the most powerful of all the nations in that part of the world. He sent word to Sennacherib that he would not resist his rule, but pay whatever the Assyrian king asked.

Sennacherib immediately laid on Hezekiah and his people a tax heavier than before. All the gold and silver in the Temple, his palace, and among the people did not satisfy Sennacherib. He sent a message threatening to destroy Jerusalem and take the people of Judah into another land, as he had done with the Israelites. The king taunted, "The gods of other nations have not been able to save them. Your God cannot save you. Surrender and go where we send you."

Fear came over Hezekiah. He took the message into the house of the Lord and spread it out before the altar. He called on God to help him save his people, then sent his princes to the prophet Isaiah to ask some word from the Lord.

Isaiah said, "The Lord says, 'The king of Assyria shall not come to this city, nor shoot an arrow against it. He shall go back to his own land the same way he came. I will cause him to fall by the sword in his own land. I will defend this city and save it, for my own sake and for my servant David's sake.'"

Just at that time, Sennacherib that heard a great army marched against him from another land. He turned from Judah to meet the new enemies. The Lord sent a sudden and terrible plague on the Assyrian army. Nearly 200,000 died in their camp one night. King Sennacherib hurried home and troubled Judah no more.

GOD SPARES HEZEKIAH
2 Kings 20

In the midst of great danger from the Assyrians, King Hezekiah was stricken with a deadly, incurable disease. Isaiah told him to set his house in order and prepare to leave his kingdom. The king felt he could not be spared. He had no son to take charge of the kingdom. Hezekiah asked that the Lord would allow him to live. "Remember how I have walked before you in truth and with a perfect heart," he prayed. "Let me live, Lord!"

God heard Hezekiah's prayer. He sent Isaiah back to the king with the message, "I have heard your prayer. I have seen your tears. I will heal you, and in three days you shall go up to the house of the Lord. I will add fifteen years to your life and save this city from the king of Assyria."

Hezekiah asked what sign God would give to show he would be cured. A sundial stood near the palace to show the time of day for there were no clocks then. Isaiah answered, "You shall choose the sign. Shall the shadow on the dial go forward ten degrees or go back ten degrees?"

"It is easy for the shadow to go forward," Hezekiah said. "Let it go back."

Isaiah called on the Lord, who heard him. He made the shadow go backward ten degrees on the sundial. Within three days Hezekiah was made well. He went to worship in the house of the Lord and lived fifteen years in honor. When the good king died, all the land mourned for him.

JEREMIAH
Jeremiah 24, 37-39

The Lord gave the prophet Jeremiah a vision of two baskets of figs. One held fresh, ripe fruit; the other, decayed figs not fit to eat. God told Jeremiah the good figs were those people who had been taken captive to Babylon. He promised to care for them and give them a heart to know Him. He said the bad figs were those left in the land, oppressed by war, the king, famine, and plague.

This vision showed Jeremiah that the captives in Babylon were the hope of the nation. He sent a message to them encouraging them to build houses, to plant, and to marry. After seventy years they would again come to their own land. He added God's promise, "My thoughts are thoughts of peace and kindness toward you. You shall call on me and I will hear you. You shall seek me and find me, when you seek me with all your heart."

Jeremiah was put into prison and left to die because he chastised King Zedekiah for turning from the Lord to idols. A kind Ethiopian let a rope down into the dungeon, drew Jeremiah up and took him to a safe, dry place in the prison. Later King Nebuchadnezzar, who was friendly to the prophet, released him. After that, Jeremiah was taken down to Egypt by enemies of the king. There he died. Because of his sad life, Jeremiah is often called the weeping prophet.

DANIEL AND HIS FRIENDS
Book of Daniel

Daniel and three friends from Judah were carried away as captives to Chaldea (Babylon) by the armies of King Nebuchadnezzar. The king renamed the friends Shadrach, Meshach, and Abednego and ordered them and Daniel to learn the language and customs of their new land.

After three years, they were taken to the palace to stand before the king. As a special honor, they were given food and wine from the king's own table. All four refused to eat and drink it. They felt to do so would be to worship idols, for the food and drink had been offerings to the images of wood and stone.

The chief of the nobles warned the young men that the king would be angry with them and him. They would not be healthy if they did not eat the food given them.

Daniel said, "Give us vegetables, bread, and water for ten days. See if we do not look healthy at that time."

The chief of the nobles liked Daniel, so he agreed. When they stood before the king ten days later, they were healthier than all the other young men and he gave them worthy places in the kingdom.

Many important things happened to Daniel and his friends. He interpreted dreams for the king. He warned that Nebuchadnezzar's kingdom would flourish, then fall, at last to be replaced by the kingdom of God Himself. He interpreted a dream that one day King Nebuchadnezzar would live with the beasts of the field and eat grass with them, but after seven years, he would be restored. Everything Daniel prophesied came true.

Once Shadrach, Meshach, and Abednego refused to bow down to the great golden idol set up on the plain. They were cast into a fiery furnace, made hotter than ever before.

Instead of burning up, the young men walked freely in

the middle of it and a fourth figure walked with them! Even King Nebuchadnezzar knew God had sent an angel to save their lives.

Daniel later interpreted a dream for Belshazzar, who saw a great hand writing words no one understood on the wall during a feast. Daniel told the king he had been weighed in the balance and found wanting. His kingdom would be given to the Medes and Persians. Before the banquet ended, it came to pass. Belshazzar's enemies burst into the palace and killed him in the midst of his feast.

Every day Daniel went to his window and prayed three times to the Lord, even though it was against the law. Although the new King Darius loved Daniel, he sadly ordered him thrown to the lions. All night long, Darius neither ate nor slept. When morning came, he rushed to the lion's den and broke the great seal, crying, "Daniel, servant of the living God, has your God been able to keep you safe from the lions?"

Out of darkness Daniel said, "King, live forever! God has sent his angel and shut the lions' mouths because the Lord saw I had done no wrong." How Darius rejoiced! He made a law that all in the land must fear and worship the Lord God, the only one who could save men. Daniel lived several years after being in the lions' den. He had many visions about the future, including the coming of Jesus.

ESTHER
Book of Esther

One of the bravest women in the Bible is Queen Esther, a Jewish girl who saved her people at risk of losing her own life. In those days, even a queen could not approach the king, except at his invitation. If she did and he refused to hold out his golden scepter to her, she would be killed.

Esther could not let her people be destroyed by the wickedness of a powerful man named Haman. So she dressed in royal robes and bravely went to the king. He held out his golden scepter and welcomed her. "What do you wish?" he asked. "It shall be given to you, even half my kingdom."

Esther invited the king and Haman to a dinner, then a second one. She exposed Haman's trickery and pleaded for the lives of her people. King Ahasuerus had Haman hanged on the very gallows he had built for another! He also permitted the Jews to defend themselves against those who tried to harm them. This brought joy and gladness to the people and they made a feast called Purim.

Jewish people still keep the feast of thanksgiving called Purim each year and read the story of Esther, the beautiful queen who saved her people.

EZRA
Book of Ezra

Ninety years after the Jews came back to their land, Jerusalem was a small town. Many of its old houses lay in ruins and it had no wall around it. At that time God raised up two men to help His people: Ezra and Nehemiah.

The priest Ezra lived in the city of Babylon, a prophet through whom God spoke to his people. Above all, Ezra loved God's book in a time when the book of the Lord had almost been forgotten. Nearly all the Old Testament books had been written long before, each copy written separately with a pen. Only a few copies existed and they were in different places.

No one before Ezra owned or had seen the whole Old Testament in one book.

The priest searched everywhere for copies of the different books. Each time he found one, he wrote a copy and kept it. He had other men copy the books they found until he had copies of all the books in the Old Testament, except the very last ones. They were written much as we have them now, except Ezra's copies were in Hebrew, the language of the men who wrote most of the Old Testament.

Ezra made one book out of the many. This great book was written on long rolls of parchment or sheepskin, as was the custom. When finished, people called it the Book of the Law for it contained God's law for His people given by Moses, Samuel, David, Isaiah, and all the other prophets.

Ezra took this book of the law from Babylon to Judea, along with men he had taught to love the law. They made copies of the book of the law, studied, and taught it to others and were called "scribes," which means writers. Ezra also taught the Jewish people they were people of God and must live apart from other nations so they would not fall into idol worship but be exact in obeying God's laws.

NEHEMIAH
Book of Nehemiah

Nehemiah the Jew was the second man God raised up to do His work at that time. A nobleman of high rank, he served as cupbearer and friend to King Artaxerxes, who ruled after Ahasuerus, the king who chose Esther as his queen. Nehemiah had a great love for

Jerusalem. It saddened him when he learned that people looked down on what had been a great city, because of its broken walls and burned gates. He asked God to help him receive grace in the king's sight, that he might do good and help his people in the land of Israel.

A few days later, the king asked, "Why do you look so sad, Nehemiah? You do not seem to be sick."

His faithful cupbearer told him, "Let the king live forever! Why should my face not be sad when the city where my fathers are buried lies waste, its walls broken and its gates burned with fire?"

"Tell me what I can do to help you," the king replied.

Nehemiah silently prayed then said, "May it please the king, I would be glad if you would send me to Jerusalem with an order to build the walls." The king not only gave permission for Nehemiah to be away for a long time, he issued letters for safe passage and authority for his servant to cut wood for a house, for repairing the Temple, and for building the wall.

Nehemiah, a company of horsemen and many friends journeyed almost 1000 miles from Persia to Jerusalem. He found the city of his fathers in even worse ruin than he expected and sadness swept over him in spite of the people's welcome. One night he slipped away from his companions, took just a few friends, and rode around the city. The next day he called the city rulers and chief priests together and said, "You see how poor and helpless the city is without walls and gates. It is open to all its enemies. Come, let us build the wall of Jerusalem, so people won't hold us in contempt."

The people joined with Nehemiah and the rulers. Almost everyone helped build the wall. They worked so hard, they completed the gigantic task in fifty-two days! Jerusalem once again began to rise from weakness to strength. When the wall was finished, Nehemiah summoned all the Jews from cities and villages to come to Jerusalem. The good priest Ezra was there at the time. He brought the great rolls on which the law was written and read it to the multitude. Nehemiah said, "This day is holy to the Lord. Be glad."

After the reading of the law, another meeting was held. The people confessed their sins and their fathers' sins in forsaking God. They solemnly vowed to keep all the commandments of God and to do His will. Nehemiah returned to his cupbearing position and did not visit Jerusalem for many years. When he did, he sadly discovered that not all the people had kept their vows to God. Working and buying and selling on the Sabbath had become common.

Nehemiah warned the people of God's anger toward those who did such things. He ordered the gates of the city to be shut before sunset on the evening before the Sabbath and not reopened until the morning after the Sabbath ended. Merchants brought their wares to the gates but Nehemiah told them to be gone. "If you come here again on the Sabbath, I will put you in prison," he shouted. By strong acts like these he led his people back to faithful service of the Lord.

THE VISION OF ZACHARIAS
Luke 1

At the time the story called the New Testament begins, the first of several Herods who ruled the land of Israel, also called Judea, sat on the throne. King Herod reported directly to Augustus Caesar, emperor at Rome.

People filled the homeland of the Jews. Cities ranged

up and down the land, Jerusalem was the largest. There Herod had begun to rebuild the Temple of the Lord to replace the old Temple built so long ago.

One day, an old priest named Zacharias was leading the worship service in the Temple. An angel appeared before him. He told Zacharias, "Do not be afraid. I bring you good news from the Lord. Your wife Elisabeth shall have a son. You are to name him John and he shall go before the Lord in the power of Elijah." He told the priest many more wonderful things.

"How shall I know your words are true?" Zacharias asked. "I am an old man and my wife is old."

"I am Gabriel, who stands in God's presence," the angel said. "Because you did not believe my words, you shall be made dumb until this comes to pass." The angel vanished and from that moment, Zacharias could not speak.

MARY AND THE ANGEL
Luke 1

E lisabeth praised the Lord when she learned she would bear a child. About six months after Zacharias saw the angel in the Temple, Gabriel appeared to Mary, a young girl in Nazareth, cousin to Elisabeth. Mary would soon marry a carpenter named Joseph. How surprised she was when Gabriel told her that God had chosen her to be the mother of a son named Jesus who would save His people from their sins. "How can this happen?" she asked.

Gabriel told Mary the Holy Spirit would come over her. He also said Elisabeth would have a child through the power of the Lord. Mary knew what she saw was real. She told the angel, "I am the servant of the Lord, to do His will. Let it be as you have said." Soon after Mary traveled to her cousin's home. Elisabeth met her at the door, crying with the Spirit of the Lord, "Blessed are you among women, and blessed among men shall be your son! Why is it the mother of my Lord comes to visit me?"

Mary sang praises and stayed with Elizabeth for nearly three months.

When Elizabeth delivered her son, Zacharias wrote, "His name is John." His speech came back and he praised God saying, "You, O child, shall be called a prophet of the Most High, to go before the Lord and make ready His ways." John grew and later went into the desert, staying until time for him to come preach to the people. The child became the great prophet John the Baptist.

THE BIRTH OF JESUS
Matthew 1; Luke 2

Joseph, the carpenter, felt troubled, but God sent a dream. In it an angel told him Mary's son would be by the Lord God. The angel said, "You are to marry her and call His name Jesus, which means salvation." Soon after their marriage, Augustus Caesar ordered all the people to report to the cities of their families to be taxed and counted. Joseph and Mary went from Nazareth to Bethlehem.

The inn was filled to overflowing. The best shelter available was a stable. There Jesus was born, lovingly wrapped, and laid in a manger.

That same night shepherds in the fields saw a wondrous light. Angels sang and announced the birth of Jesus at the stable. When the glory faded, the shepherds rose and went to Bethlehem. They found Mary and Joseph and Jesus, just as the angels had said. Mary said nothing when the shepherds fell to the ground and worshipped her newborn son, telling of the angel song. She kept all these things in her heart and the shepherds went back to their flocks, praising God.

Mary and Joseph named the baby Jesus, and when He was eight days old, they took Him to the Temple to make an offering. A man of God named Simeon had been promised he would not die before seeing the Christ. When Simeon took Jesus in his arms, he lifted his voice in praise. He also prophesied to Mary, "Sorrow like a sword will pierce your heart." She did not know at that time one day Jesus would die on a cross and her own heart would nearly break from pain.

THE WISE MEN
Matthew 2

Remaining in Bethlehem, Mary and Joseph and the baby Jesus found a house to live in. Sometime later, strange men from a faraway land east of Judea came to see them. "Where is he that is born King of the Jews?" they asked King Herod. "We have seen His star and followed it that we might worship Him."

Their visit made the old king very angry. A new king, one to displace him on the throne? He called his advisors and learned that the promised king would be born in Bethlehem! Herod told the wise men he also wanted to worship and asked them to let him know when they found the child.

God showed the wise men Herod's trickery. They presented gifts of gold, frankincense, and myrrh (precious perfumes) to Jesus, then went to their own country another way. Soon after, God sent another dream to Joseph. An angel warned him to take Jesus and Mary to Egypt, for Herod sought to find and kill the child. The little family didn't even wait until morning, but fled in the night.

Herod ordered his soldiers to kill all the children under two years of age, but Mary, Joseph, and Jesus lived safely in Egypt until an angel told them that King Herod had died and they could go back to their own land. They arrived to find that the successor to the throne was as cruel as his father, so Joseph took his family to Nazareth in another part of Galilee.

JESUS IN THE TEMPLE
Luke 2

"Where is Jesus?" Mary asked Joseph on their way home from the Feast of the Passover in Jerusalem. "I thought he was with our kinsmen but I cannot find him anywhere." A thorough search of the caravan revealed that Jesus was not among the travelers. Mary and Joseph hurried back to Jerusalem and frantically went from friend to relative. They still did not find their twelve-year-old son.

On the third day, they went up to the Temple with heavy hearts. There sat Jesus with the teachers of the law, asking questions that amazed all those present. Mary sagged with relief, then demanded, "Child, why have you treated us so? Your father and I have been looking for you and were worried."

"Why?" Jesus asked. "Didn't you know I would be in my Father's house?"

They did not understand and Jesus immediately rose and went with them. He grew from boy to young man, strong of body and with a keen, inquiring mind. He earned the love of those about him. He also learned the carpenter trade. When Joseph died, Jesus as oldest son took care of His mother, brothers, and sisters.

Work, quiet life in a country village, and worship at the synagogue kept Him busy and the years passed until Jesus was thirty years old.

JOHN
Luke 3

News swept throughout the land. A prophet had come from the wilderness to give the people the word of the Lord in power and might! More than 400 years had passed since God had sent a prophet. Now one spoke what God told him, instead of what he had learned from old writings. People flocked to hear him.

John, son of Zacharias and Elisabeth, had no beauty. He wore rough clothing of camel hair. He preached, "Repent, for the kingdom of heaven is at hand. If a man has two coats, let him give one to him that has none. He that has more food than he needs, let him give to him that is hungry." Day after day John baptized people in the Jordan River as a sign their sins were washed away.

Some asked, "Is John the Christ God promised to send to rule His people?"

"Nay," John told them. "I baptize with water. One comes after me who is so high above me I am not fit to stoop and loosen the strings of His shoes. He shall baptize you with the Holy Spirit and fire."

One day Jesus, the young Nazareth carpenter, came seeking baptism. John recognized His greatness and holiness, "You come to me, when I have need to be baptized by You?"

Jesus answered, "Let it be so. It is fitting that I do all things that are right."

John baptized Jesus. As Jesus came out of the water and was praying, the heavens opened. The Holy Spirit in the form of a dove rested on Him. A voice from heaven said, "This is my beloved Son, in whom I am well pleased." John knew at that moment Jesus was the Son of God, the long-awaited Christ.

JESUS CALLS DISCIPLES
Luke 4, 6; John 1

For forty days after Jesus was baptized, He stayed alone in the desert seeking God and planning the work He must do. He did not eat or drink. Neither did He listen when Satan tempted Him with food, power, and glory. Finally, Satan gave up and angels brought the food Jesus needed after his long fast.

A short time later, John the Baptist saw Jesus coming toward him. He said, "Behold the Lamb of God, who takes away the sin of the world! This is the Son of God." The next day two of John's followers stood with him. Again Jesus walked by and John repeated what he had said the day before. The young men Andrew and John spoke with Jesus and asked where he stayed so they could speak with Him.

"Come and see," Jesus said. The men listened to His

words and went away knowing Jesus was the Saviour and King of Israel. Andrew ran to his brother Peter and exclaimed, "We have found the Anointed One, the Christ, who is to be the King of Israel." He brought Peter to meet Jesus.

Without waiting to hear Peter's name, Jesus told him, "Your name is Simon, the son of Jonas. I give you a new name: Peter, the rock." Sometimes Peter's Hebrew name is used, and he is called Cephas, which also means rock. Peter immediately followed Jesus. So did others, until Jesus had twelve special men who walked with him and were called disciples.

WHAT JESUS DID
John 2, 4-5; Matthew 9, 12;
Mark 2; Luke 2-6

Jesus' first miracle was turning water to wine at a wedding in Cana. His mother felt sorry when the wine ran out, a shameful thing to happen at a feast. Jesus ordered large jars of water brought and filled with water. He told the servants to draw out and serve. It had been turned to wine, finer than any previously served!

At the Feast of the Passover, Jesus found men selling oxen, sheep, and doves in the Temple. Others sat changing money. Jesus picked up a cord and made a little whip. He drove out the buyers and sellers, the sheep and oxen. He overturned the tables and said, "Take these things away! My Father's house shall not be a house of buying and selling!"

This did not please the Jews, many of whom grew rich from Temple selling. "What right do you have to come in here and do these things?" they shouted.

"I will give you a sign. Destroy this house of God and in three days I will raise it up." (He spoke not of the Temple, but meant when they put Him to death, He would rise again in three days. Later His followers remembered and understood.)

A ruler of the Jews named Nicodemus came to Jesus by night. "Master, we know You are a teacher from God. No man can do what you do."

Jesus said, "Unless a man is born again, he cannot see the kingdom of God." When Nicodemus asked what this meant, Jesus replied, "Unless a man is born of water and of the Spirit, he cannot enter into the kingdom of God." Jesus meant we must be baptized and receive God's Spirit in us to become His children.

Another time, Jesus came to a village well, thirsty but without a rope to draw up water. He asked a Samaritan woman to give Him a drink. She looked shocked. "You, a Jew, ask a Samaritan woman for a drink?"

Jesus promised her God had a free gift, living water. Once she drank of it, she need never thirst again. She didn't understand, but wanted the living water. Jesus told her to bring her husband. She had none. He said, "You have spoken truth. You have had five husbands and the man you now have is not your husband."

The Samaritan woman was so filled with wonder she listened to Jesus' teachings. He told her that He was the Christ. She ran to the village and brought as many people as would come to hear him. Many believed Him to be the Saviour.

A nobleman of Capernaum heard of Jesus. He rode all night to ask Jesus to heal his dying son. He arrived home and discovered the child began to get better at the exact moment Jesus had told him, "Your son will live."

Jesus got so much attention, it made enemies of those who were jealous and feared he would take away their power. He read prophecies from Isaiah in the synagogue, then told them He was the One of whom the scriptures spoke. They began to murmur, "Is not this the son of the carpenter Joseph? Why doesn't He do miracles here instead of somewhere far off?"

Jesus knew their thoughts and sadly told them, "No prophet has honor among his own people." Because of their disbelief, there would be no miracles. They dragged Jesus outdoors and would have thrown him to his death, but He quietly slipped out of their hands and went away. It was not yet time for Him to die.

Simon Peter and Andrew had fished all night and caught nothing. After Jesus finished preaching to the people on the seashore, He told His friends, "Launch out into the deep and let down your nets." They obeyed and caught so many fish the boat nearly sank! Jesus told them, "Follow me and I will make you fishers of men." From then on, Simon, Andrew, James, and John left their fishing and walked with Jesus as His disciples.

Jesus went throughout the land, healing many afflictions: evil spirits, palsy, even leprosy. Chief rulers tried to trick Him. They condemned Him for healing a man on the Sabbath. Jesus ignored them and continued doing His Father's will.

JESUS AND THE TEMPLE RULERS
Mark 11; Matthew 21

Early Monday morning, Jesus led His disciples over the Mount of Olives toward Jerusalem and went to the Temple, where He had driven out the sellers and the money changers three years before. Now he found the traders there again, selling oxen, sheep, and doves for sacrifices and changing money at the tables.

Again Jesus turned over the tables and cleared out the sellers. He told the people, "It is written in the prophets, 'My house shall be called a house of prayer for all nations,' but you have made it a den of thieves!" This made the Temple rulers furious.

The Jews allowed no blind or lame persons in the Temple. But they forgot that God looks at hearts, not bodies. Jesus found many at the doors of the Temple who needed healing. He allowed them to enter and healed them. The little children who loved Jesus saw Him in the Temple and cried out, as did others, "Hosanna to the Son of David!" The chief priests and scribes were greatly displeased but Jesus told them perfect praise came out of the mouths of babes and little ones.

The common people flocked to hear Jesus' plain and simple teachings. This made the rulers even angrier. They wanted to kill him, but dared not because of the crowd. That night Jesus went back to Bethany where He was safe.

THE WEDDING FEAST
Matthew 22

On Tuesday, Jesus told the people a parable that we call the Wedding Feast. "A certain king made a great feast at the wedding of his son. He sent his servant to bring the guests. They would not come. He sent other servants, telling those invited that dinner was all ready. Still they did not come. One went to his farm, another to his shop. Others seized the servants, beat, and even killed some of them.

"This made the king very angry. He ordered the murderers killed and their city burned. He told his servants to go into the streets and bring in everyone they could find rich, poor, high, low, good, bad and tell them they were welcome. Soon all the places were filled. All who came received a wedding garment so they would be dressed properly for the king.

"One man wouldn't wear a wedding garment. The king ordered him bound and thrown out into the darkness." Jesus added, "For in the kingdom of God many are called, but few are chosen."

"GIVE TO CAESAR"
Matthew 22

Jesus' enemies sent spies to trick Him. On one occasion they asked, "Should the Jews pay taxes to the Roman Emperor Caesar?"

Jesus took a coin, held it up and asked. "Whose head and name are inscribed on the coin?"

"Caesar, the Roman emperor," they said.

Jesus outwitted them, as usual. "Give Caesar the things that are Caesar's and give God the things that are God's," Jesus commanded.

He had more to say about money. He watched people dropping their gifts of money in the Temple treasury. The rich threw in great sums, proud to be seen as generous. One poor widow dropped in two coins whose value only amounted to a quarter of a cent. Jesus said, "This poor widow has given more than all the other people. They gave from their plenty; she cast in all she had." He left the Temple, never again to enter.

THE PASSOVER FEAST
Luke 22, John 13

"Where shall we make ready the Passover for You to eat?" the disciples asked Jesus.

He called Peter and John and said, "Go into the city. Follow a man carrying a pitcher of water. Go into the house where he goes and say, 'The Master says, "Where is my guest room? Where can I eat the Passover with my disciples?"'" He will show you a large furnished upper room. Make it ready for us."

Peter and John obeyed. They went out, bought a lamb and roasted it. They prepared the vegetables and thin wafers of bread used for the Passover meal.

During the meal, Jesus gave thanks, broke bread and poured wine. He told them it represented His broken body and spilled blood. They were to eat, drink, and always remember the sacrifice He made so their sins could be forgiven.

Jesus knelt and washed the disciples' feet, as though he were a servant. Peter objected. "Lord, You will never wash my feet." When Jesus told Peter if He did not wash him, Peter would not be His disciple, impulsive Peter replied, "Lord, don't just wash my feet, but my hands and head, too!"

Jesus said, "One who has already bathed only needs to wash his feet, then he is clean." He grew sorrowful. "One of you who eats with me shall betray me and give me up to those who will kill me."

"Is it I, Lord?" the disciples asked.

Jesus dipped a piece of bread into the dish and gave it to Judas Iscariot. He said, "Do quickly what you are going to do." Not all heard Jesus. Those who did thought Jesus was telling him to do something about the feast or the money he carried. Judas slipped away to the rulers. His plan must be done now or never.

"I must leave you for a time. You cannot come where I am. Remember my new commandment," Jesus said. "Love one another even as I have loved you."

"Where are you going?" Peter asked. "I will lay down my life for Your sake."

Jesus said, "Peter, before the cock crows tomorrow morning, you will three times deny you ever knew me."

Peter stubbornly continued to insist he would never deny the Lord. About midnight, they left the upper room and went to the Mount of Olives.

BETRAYAL
Matthew 26, Luke 22

At the foot of the Mount of Olives, near the path to Bethany, an orchard of olive trees was called the Garden of Gethsemane. Jesus left eight of his disciples outside. He took Peter, James, and John into the orchard, telling them to keep watch while He prayed. Jesus knew in a little while Judas would come with a band of men to seize Him. Now was the time to prepare for His final time on earth. Jesus suffered so much as He prayed, great drops of sweat fell like blood.

"O, my Father," he cried. "If it be possible, let this cup pass away from me. Nevertheless, not as I will, but as You will!" He went to His disciples and found them asleep. "Could you not watch with me one hour?" He asked, then went back into the woods alone and again sought His Father in heaven.

A second time Jesus found His three disciples sleeping, but He did not awaken them. He left them and prayed, using the same words. An angel came from heaven and gave Jesus strength. This time when He went to His disciples, He said, "Rise up. The traitor is here."

Judas stood in the midst of flashing torches, gleaming swords, and spears.

When he bargained with the enemy for thirty pieces of silver, Judas promised to kiss Jesus to show which one He was. Now He did this.

"Who do you seek?" Jesus' voice rang out in the night.

"Jesus of Nazareth," came the reply.

"I am He."

The throng fell back with fear, but after the second time Jesus asked the question and identified Himself, they came forward to take Him. Peter angrily drew his sword and cut off the right ear of one of the men, but Jesus told Him to put up his sword. He touched the place where the ear had been cut off and instantly it came on again and the man was well.

When the disciples saw that Jesus would not let them fight for Him, they ran away. The enemy bound Jesus and led Him to the house of the high priest. Peter and John followed the crowd. John went inside the high priest's house, but Peter stayed outside, warming himself at a charcoal fire in the courtyard.

A maid said to Peter, "You were with Jesus of Nazareth."

Afraid to admit the truth, Peter said, "Woman, I do not know the man." Twice more he said the same thing, cursing and denying his Master. The next moment, Peter heard the shrill crow of a cock. He also saw Jesus being dragged from the hall of the high priest Annas to the other high priest, Caiaphas, his son-in-law.

Jesus turned and looked at Peter. The fisherman remembered what Jesus had said about denying his Lord. Peter ran into the night, weeping bitterly.

JESUS ON TRIAL
Luke 22-23

After Jesus first told Annas He had spoken only the truth and no evil, He did not speak to either high priest until Caiaphas demanded, "Are you Christ, the Son of God?"

The world waited for His answer. Jesus flung up His head, gaze fixed on his persecutor. "I am. You will one day see the Son of man sitting on the throne of power and coming in the clouds of heaven!"

"He says He is the Son of God," Caiaphas shrieked. "Blasphemy!"

"He must be put to death," the assembled rulers of the Jews screamed. They mocked him and spat on Him, then voted for His death. However, they had no authority to execute anyone. Only Pontius Pilate, the Roman governor, could do that. So all the rulers and a great multitude took Jesus to Pilate's castle.

Until this time, Judas did not really believe Jesus would be put to death. Perhaps he thought the Master would save Himself, as He had others. When he learned that Jesus did not protect Himself, Judas hurried back to those with whom he had made the bargain to betray Jesus. "I have sinned," he cried.

"What is that to us?" they jeered. They would not take the thirty pieces of silver back and free Jesus. Wild with pain and remorse, Judas ran to the Temple. He threw the money on the floor, then went out and hanged himself.

The rulers could not put the betrayal price into the treasury. They bought a piece of ground called a potter's field and set it apart for burying strangers who might die in Jerusalem. Everyone in the city called it the Field of Blood.

Pilate wanted nothing to do with Jesus. He found no fault in Him. When he learned that Jesus came from Galilee, Pilate smiled to himself and ordered Jesus to be taken to Herod, who ruled Galilee and happened to be in Jerusalem at the time.

Herod had never forgotten John the Baptist. He refused to take responsibility for the death of another prophet. When Jesus neither performed miracles nor answered Herod's questions, the ruler had Him dressed in a robe as though He were a make-believe king and sent Him back to Pilate.

Pilate's wife sent him a message. "Do nothing against that good man. I suffered many things in a dream on account of Him." Pilate wanted to set Jesus free, as was the custom at the feast. The crowd roared, "Set the robber Barabbas free! Crucify Jesus!" Pilate called for water, washed his hands in front of all and said, "My hands are clean from the blood of this good man." Then he gave orders that Jesus, a man he knew was innocent of all wrongdoing, be crucified."

THE DEATH OF JESUS
Luke 23; John 19; Mark 15; Matthew 27

The Roman soldiers took Jesus, beat Him again and led him out of the city to a place called Golgotha in the Jewish language, Calvary in that of the Romans. Both words mean the Skull Place. They tried to make Jesus carry his heavy cross, but He fell and could not, so they compelled a man named Simon to carry it for Him.

At Calvary, the soldiers nailed Jesus to the cross. They placed a sign written in three different languages over His head: Jesus, King of the Jews. The multitude mocked Him. The soldiers gambled for His robe at the foot of the cross. Even in His agony, Jesus prayed for the soldiers, "Father forgive them. They know not what they are doing."

Robbers hung on crosses on either side of Jesus. One said, "If you are the Christ, save Yourself and us."

The other robber cried, "Have you no fear of God, to speak so? We deserve to die. This man has done nothing wrong." He looked at Jesus. "Lord, remember me when You come into Your kingdom!"

Jesus answered, "Today you shall be with me in heaven."

Mary, Jesus' mother, and other women stood below the cross. Jesus gave his mother into John's keeping. About noon, sudden darkness fell. It lasted for three hours. After six hours of terrible agony, Jesus called, "My God, why have You forsaken me?"

He spoke again: "I thirst." Instead of water, someone gave Him vinegar. Jesus said, "It is finished. Father, into thy hands I give my spirit," and He died. At that exact moment, the veil in the Temple tore from top to bottom and a great earthquake came. The Roman officer in charge of the soldiers around the cross burst out, "Truly this man was the Son of God!

To be sure Jesus was dead, a soldier ran a spear into His body. Both water and blood came out of the wound. Nicodemus and Joseph of Arimathea went to Pilate and asked for the body of Jesus. Pilate agreed. The men sadly took Jesus from the cross and wrapped Him in fine linen. They placed Him in Joseph's own new tomb and rolled a great rock in front.

The next morning some of the rulers came to Pilate. "Jesus said He would rise after three days. Give orders for the tomb to be sealed and guarded, lest the disciples steal the body and say Jesus is risen." It was done as they asked.

EASTER
Matthew 28; Mark 16; Luke 24; John 20-21

On Sunday morning, some women went to the tomb at daybreak. They found the seal broken, the stone rolled away and no sign of the guards. They did not know there had been an earthquake. Or that an angel had rolled away the stone and sat on it. It frightened the guards so much, they fell to the ground as though dead. As soon as they could get up, they fled in terror.

Mary Magdalene ran to tell the disciples. The other women looked inside. Two angels sat there, but Jesus' body was missing. "Do not be afraid," an angel said. "Jesus is not here, but risen. Go tell His disciples and Peter that Jesus will go before you into Galilee. You will see Him there."

Mary Magdalene, in the meantime, found Peter and John. They hurried to the tomb; it lay empty and still. The disciples left, but Mary Magdalene remained, weeping over the loss of her master.

"Woman, why do you weep?" a voice asked.

Mary thought the man speaking was the gardener. She answered, "Because they have taken away my Lord. I do not know where they have laid Him. Sir, if you have carried Him out of this place, tell me where you have laid Him."

"Mary," said the stranger.

Jesus! When He spoke her name, Mary knew Jesus' voice and fell before Him, reaching to touch His feet. "Master!"

"Do not take hold of me," Jesus told her. "I am not yet going away to my Father. Go to my brothers and say to them, I go up to my Father, and to your Father, to my God, and your God."

Later, Jesus appeared to others: some of the women; Peter; Cleopas and some disciples who were walking from Jerusalem to Emmaus. They didn't recognize Jesus until He tarried with them for the evening meal, then vanished. The two men rushed back to Jerusalem. They found all the remaining disciples except Thomas, gathered together. Suddenly Jesus appeared in the room, although the doors were shut. They thought Him a spirit, but He showed them His hands and side, then he ate some bread and honeycomb. How they rejoiced!

Thomas listened to the other disciples' story of seeing Jesus, but said he would not believe until he saw and touched the nailprints in Jesus' feet and the wound in His side. A week later, Jesus again appeared in the middle of the room. He told Thomas to come touch Him and have faith.

Thomas said, "My Lord and my God!"

"Because you have seen, you have believed," Jesus said. "Blessed are they that have not seen and yet have believed."

Inspirational Library

Beautiful purse/pocket size editions of Christian classics bound in flexible leatherette. These books make thoughtful gifts for everyone on your list, including yourself!

> *The Bible Promise Book*   Over 1000 promises from God's Word arranged by topic. What does God promise about matters like: Anger, Illness, Jealousy, Love, Money, Old Age, and Mercy? Find out in this book!
> Flexible Leatherette . . . .
> $3.97

> *Wisdom from the Proverbs*   Daily thoughts from Proverbs which communicate truths about ourselves and the world around us.
> Flexible Leatherette . . . .
> $4.97

> *My Daily Prayer Journal*   Each page is dated and features a Scripture verse and ample room for you to record your thoughts, prayers, and praises. One page for each day of the year.
> Flexible Leatherette . . . .
> $4.97

Available wherever books are sold.
Or order from:

Barbour Publishing, Inc.
P.O. Box 719
Uhrichsville, OH 44683
http://www.barbourbooks.com

If you order by mail add $2.00 to your order for shipping.
Prices subject to change without notice.